Vocabulary Power Plus

Vocabulary, Reading, and Writing Exercises
for Higher Achievement

Level Seven

By Daniel A. Reed

Edited by Mary Beardsley

ISBN   978-1-58049-266-9

Prestwick House

P.O. Box 658 · Clayton, DE 19938
(800) 932-4593 · www.prestwickhouse.com

D1115769

Table of Contents

Introduction 5

Strategies for Completing Activities 6

Pronunciation Guide. 11

Word List 12

Lesson One 17

Lesson Two 25

Lesson Three 33

Review: Lessons 1-3 41

Lesson Four. 45

Lesson Five 53

Lesson Six 61

Review: Lessons 4-6 69

Lesson Seven 73

Lesson Eight 81

Lesson Nine. 89

Review: Lessons 7-9 97

Lesson Ten 101

Lesson Eleven 109

Lesson Twelve. 117

Review: Lessons 10-12 125

Lesson Thirteen. 129

Lesson Fourteen 137

Lesson Fifteen. 145

Review: Lessons 13-15 153

Lesson Sixteen. 157

Lesson Seventeen 165

Lesson Eighteen 173

Review: Lessons 16-18 181

Lesson Nineteen 185

Lesson Twenty 193

Lesson Twenty-One 201

Review Lessons 19-21. 209

INTRODUCTION

Vocabulary *Power Plus* Levels Six through Eight combine classroom-tested vocabulary drills with reading exercises designed to prepare students for both secondary school and the revised Scholastic Assessment Test; however, *Vocabulary Power Plus* is a resource for all students—not just those who are college bound or preparing for the SAT. This series is intended to increase vocabulary, improve grammar, enhance writing, and boost critical reading skills for students at all levels of learning.

Vocabulary Power Plus reinforces each vocabulary word by presenting it in several different contexts. Words in Context activities allow students to identify the correct context for each lesson's words. Sentence Completion and Improving Paragraphs exercises foster writing and editing skills and prompt students to create contexts for words instead of simply memorizing definitions. Each exercise, including Prefixes and Suffixes and Reading Comprehension, is linked to the vocabulary list. Students receive additional reinforcement through review activities after every third lesson. Review lessons further the development of inference skills and highlight word relationships and shades of meaning.

We hope that you find the *Vocabulary Power Plus* series to be an effective tool for teaching new words and an exceptional tool for preparing students for secondary school and standardized tests.

Strategies for Completing Activities

Words in Context

To complete the answer for Words in Context questions, first read the entire sentence, and then focus on the words closest to the blank and determine the correct answer's part of speech.

If a noun precedes the blank, then the answer is likely to be a verb. For example:

> The repairman _____ an old sock when he looked beneath the dryer.

In this example, *repairman* is the subject of the clause containing the blank, and *sock* is the object. The sentence would become senseless if an adjective or a noun were used in the blank.

If an adjective precedes the blank space, then the answer is most likely a noun. For example:

> The tired _____ has been fixing dryers all day long.

The adjective *tired* must modify something. Using an adjective for the answer creates a nonsensical sentence. The answer cannot be a verb because the sentence provides no subject for the verb *has been fixing*. Placing a noun in the blank creates a subject for the sentence and provides a word for *tired* to modify.

Articles such as *a, an,* and *the* can also precede nouns, but you must look at what follows the blank to determine what type of word the answer will be. For example:

> The repairman fixed a _____ today.

In this example, the blank must be a noun, which serves as the object of the verb *fixed.*

> The repairman fixed a _____ dryer today.

In this example, the blank must be an adjective, because something must modify the noun *dryer.*

An answer's part of speech varies also when a verb precedes the blank. If a verb precedes the blank, first determine the purpose of the verb. Will the answer be the *object* of the verb, or a *part* of the verb? For example:

> The repairman fixed _____ dryers today.

In this example, the answer must be an adjective that modifies *dryers*.

> The repairman plans to _____ the dryer tomorrow.

In this example, the answer will be a verb that completes the infinitive phrase, *to....*

> The repairman will not _____ the dryer today.

In this example, the answer will be a verb that completes the verb phrase, *will not....*

Identifying the answer's part of speech will allow you to narrow the word list down to a few possible answers, but you must take into account the rest of the sentence to select the answer that best matches the context of the sentence. As you read, think about the context of the answer. Does the sentence have a positive connotation, or is it negative? Is it formal, or is it casual? Does it use language specific to a particular subject or field of study that would limit the answer to a specific word?

Sentence Completion

The main thing to remember about sentence completion is that your answer must show that you understand the meaning of the word. Your answer must *show* the word in use—not simply redefine the word. For example:

> When it landed on the floor after being dropped, the *flimsy* container...

The word is *flimsy*, which means *delicate* or *fragile*. To create your answer, first ask yourself what would reveal to you whether something is *flimsy*. In this sentence, the clue is already begun for you because the flimsy container has been dropped onto the floor. Determine what a *flimsy* container would do if it fell onto the floor, and write it:

> When it landed on the floor after being dropped, the *flimsy* container...shattered into many small pieces, spilling its contents everywhere.

Prefixes and Suffixes

Use the Words in Context strategy of determining a part of speech to decide the type of word you will need to complete each sentence. You must form the word you need by combining a vocabulary word with a prefix or suffix, which means that your answer will use the same root as the vocabulary word provided, if not the entire word.

To identify the answer, first consider the definition of the given word and how it relates to the topic of the sentence provided. Then, look over the prefixes and suffixes and select the one that creates the proper part of speech and usage for the context of the answer.

Critical Reading

Reading questions generally fall into three categories:

1. *Identifying the main idea or the author's purpose.* Generally, the question will ask, "What is this selection about?"

In some passages, the author's purpose will be easy to identify because the one or two ideas leap from the text; however, other passages might not be so easily analyzed, especially if they include convoluted sentences. Inverted sentences (subject at the end of the sentence) and elliptical sentences (words missing) will also increase the difficulty of the passages, but all these obstacles can be overcome if readers take one sentence at a time and recast it in their own words. Consider the following sentence:

> *When determining an individual's total worth to the team, one must first, and perhaps most importantly, consider the player's attendance record, as this suggests important information about the individual's degree of commitment and is a significant indicator of the player's priorities, which should place the team near the top; a dependable teammate will demonstrate dedicated allegiance to the team through persistent practice and support of other players.*

If we edit out some of the words, the main point of this sentence is obvious.

> When determining an individual's   worth to the team,
>   consider the player's
> attendance record, as this
>   the individual's degree of commitment and
>   priorities
>   ; a dependable teammate will demonstrate
>   allegiance to the team through   practice
> and support of other players.

Some sentences need only a few deletions for clarification, but others require major recasting and additions; they must be read carefully and put into the reader's own words.

> Some in their discourse desire rather commendation of wit, in being able to hold all arguments, than of judgment, in discerning what is true; as if it were a praise to know what might be said, and not what should be thought.

After studying it, a reader might recast the sentence as follows:

> In conversation, some people desire praise for their abilities to maintain the conversation rather than their abilities to identify what is true or false, as though it were better to sound good than to know what is truth or fiction.

2.   *Identifying the stated or implied meaning.* What is the author stating or suggesting?

The literal meaning of a text does not always correspond with the intended meaning. To understand a passage fully, readers must determine which meaning—if there is more than one—is the intended meaning of the passage. Consider the following sentence:

> ...an expression of courtesy and interest gleamed out upon his features; proving that there was light within him and that it was only the outward medium of the intellectual lamp that obstructed the rays in their passage.

Interpreted literally, this Nathaniel Hawthorne metaphor suggests that a light-generating lamp exists inside of the human body. Since this is impossible, the reader must look to the metaphoric meaning of the passage to understand it properly. In the metaphor, Hawthorne refers to the human mind—consciousness—as a lamp that emits light, and other people cannot always see the lamp because the outside "medium"—the human body—sometimes blocks it.

3.   *Identifying the tone or mood of the selection.* What feeling does the text evoke?

To answer these types of questions, readers must look closely at words and their connotations; for example, the words *stubborn* and *firm* share almost the same definition, but a writer who describes a character as *stubborn* rather than *firm* is probably suggesting something negative about the character.

Improving Paragraphs

When you read a passage, remember that Improving Paragraphs exercises focus on the clarity and organization of the whole passage as opposed to single, confined, grammatical errors. Improving Paragraphs questions fall into four categories:

1.   *Analytical.* This type of question involves the main idea, or organization, of the passage, and it might require you to understand the purpose or the meaning of the whole passage before you answer. Be aware of topic sentences, sentences that contradict the author's intention, and information that seems to be in the wrong place.

2.   *Sentence Revision.* Revision questions focus on single, troubled sentences that either lack clarity or contain some other type of flaw. These sentences may or may not affect the whole paragraph.

3.   *Sentence Combination.* Combination questions ask you to fulfill the purpose of existing sentences using fewer words, thus simplifying and clarifying the text. These can sometimes be identified during your initial reading of the text, because flawed combinations distort meanings and create awkward paragraphs.

4.   *Sentence Addition.* Addition questions present sentences which, when added to the passage or deleted from the passage, enhance the general clarity of the text. Watch for "loose ends" or poor transitions between paragraphs as potential areas for addition questions.

Pronunciation Guide

a — track
ā — mate
ä — father
â — care
e — pet
ē — be
i — bit
ī — bite
o — job
ō — wrote
ô — port, fought
ōō — proof
ŏŏ — book
u — pun
ū — you
û — purr
ə — about, system, supper, circus
îr — steer
oi — toy

Word List

Lesson 1
articulate
crux
debris
decry
eminent
harass
milieu
opportune
refuse
skeptical
successor
sullen
trivial
tinge
unkempt

Lesson 2
belittle
blasé
concoct
decade
diverse
enunciate
hurtle
improvise
jostle
libel
mammoth
paradox
provincial
realm
undermine

Lesson 3
amity
cater
guise
inconsequential
jubilant
placate
preclude
repress
saturate
slake
sortie
succumb
tranquil
venomous
wrest

Lesson 4
acute
durable
eavesdrop
ethical
fjord
gaudy
nurture
nominal
pommel
quibble
rampart
respite
rite
seismic
terrestrial

Lesson 5
bizarre
bungle
deduce
dynamic
irrelevant
loiter
obstinate
scrutinize
stunt
superficial
ultimate
vapid
viable
wan
wane

Lesson 6
adjacent
candor
compassion
democratic
disperse
doleful
duress
irk
ratify
sobriety
stagnate
subordinate
talon
taut
wallow

Lesson 7	Lesson 9	Lesson 11
badger	antagonist	authoritarian
benevolent	detriment	avenge
elapse	drone	bewilder
fitful	drudgery	bristle
genre	horizontal	clemency
haven	hypocrite	elaborate
immaterial	insubordinate	gazebo
innate	mentor	malady
kindle	oration	mar
listless	retract	obscure
meager	sanctuary	obsolete
octogenarian	scamper	pretext
permeate	solace	teem
republic	somber	translucent
tether	zenith	transparent

Lesson 8	Lesson 10	Lesson 12
alight	brash	appall
convalesce	buff	constraint
dainty	intemperate	dissuade
feint	interrogate	falter
implore	moot	frail
impugn	opaque	hypothetical
integral	pragmatic	irate
jurisdiction	prestigious	peninsula
malnutrition	prodigy	placid
meddle	savory	prejudice
painstaking	sedate	prelude
pantheon	singular	profane
sear	spontaneous	puny
vertical	usurp	ruthless
wince	whimsical	skirmish

Lesson 13

bystander
cede
comprehensive
devout
flounder
foster
incite
pittance
precipitate
restrictive
scurry
shrewd
spew
tact
vigorous

Lesson 14

accost
ascend
candidate
conventional
culprit
daft
disparage
miscellaneous
placard
proximity
quarry
regatta
sordid
stereotype
whet

Lesson 15

arbitrary
conspicuous
detest
dexterity
dreg
flourish
fray
incoherent
nullify
paltry
persistent
prediction
sinister
succinct
tundra

Lesson 16

concise
dubious
dupe
feudal
illegible
indigent
inhibition
merit
potent
protagonist
ruse
straightforward
subsequent
vogue
writhe

Lesson 17

askew
cope
deceptive
engrossed
facilitate
gusto
premise
rejuvenate
remote
reprehensible
reverberate
speculate
supplement
vain
yen

Lesson 18

asset
construe
equilibrium
imperturbable
interloper
melancholy
petty
potential
prudent
suave
tertiary
unabated
unique
vie
wither

Lesson 19	Lesson 20	Lesson 21
adverse	assail	aspire
alliance	astute	composure
altruism	condolence	deploy
blunder	enigma	exonerate
bolster	fruitless	exploit
brazen	inexplicable	flamboyant
indifferent	malignant	fret
insurgent	monotonous	hostile
lucid	profound	lackluster
mutual	rail	maternal
quaint	shun	morose
retort	subterranean	procrastinate
technology	valor	replenish
terminal	variable	saga
vigil	virtue	static

Lesson One

1. **articulate** (är tik´ yə lit) *adj.* well-spoken; clear
   (är tik´ yə lāt) *v.* to speak clearly and distinctly
   (adj) The *articulate* woman made a living narrating for radio and television advertisements.
   (v) Please *articulate* the instructions so there is no confusion over what to do.
   (adj) *syn: eloquent; coherent*   *ant: tongue-tied; unclear*
   (v)   *syn: enunciate; pronounce*   *ant: mumble; murmur*

2. **crux** (kruks) *n.* the main or most important point or feature
   Sam's refusal to admit his responsibility was the very *crux* of the dilemma.
   syn: core; root; center

3. **debris** (də brē´) *n.* scattered remnants; rubble
   The typhoon destroyed buildings and filled the streets with *debris*.
   syn: ruins; waste

4. **decry** (dē krī´) *v.* to condemn or disapprove openly
   Citizens *decried* the new law until a court ruled it unconstitutional.
   syn: denounce; condemn   *ant: applaud; praise*

5. **eminent** (em´ ə nənt) *adj.* famous; prominent
   The *eminent* architect received numerous awards for her latest skyscraper design.
   syn: renowned; celebrated   *ant: unknown; common*

6. **harass** (hə ras´) *v.* to torment continually; to irritate
   Damian's mother *harassed* him until he finally cleaned up his room.
   syn: hound; hassle   *ant: soothe; please*

7. **milieu** (mil yoo´) *n.* an atmosphere or setting
   Frank enjoys the Victorian *milieu* of Sherlock Holmes novels.
   syn: environment; domain

8. **opportune** (op ər tōōn´) *adj.* happening at a convenient time; favorable
   Monday was the *opportune* day for the party because most of the guests had the day off.
   syn: appropriate; suitable   *ant: inappropriate; undesirable*

9. **refuse** (rē fūz´) *v.* to decline to accept or allow
   (ref´ ūs) *n.* discarded items; trash
   (v) You will not be allowed to rent any more videos if you *refuse* to pay the late fees.
   (n) All *refuse* must be taken to the city dump.
   (v) *syn: reject; deny*   *ant: accept; acknowledge*
   (n) *syn: garbage; rubbish*

10. **skeptical** (skep´ ti kəl) *adj.* doubting; disbelieving
    Dan was *skeptical* about buying a watch from the vendor on the street.
    syn: doubtful; questioning   *ant: confident; certain*

11. **successor** (sək ses´ ər) *n.* one who inherits, will inherit, or is next-in-line for a position or title
    The *successor* to the late-night talk-show host was never as funny as the original host.
    syn: heir; descendent   *ant: predecessor*

12. **sullen** (sul´ ən) *adj.* miserable; gloomy; somber
    Her *sullen* poetry reflects her real-life depression and uncertainties.
    syn: dark; dismal   *ant: cheerful; bright*

13. **tinge** (tinj) *v.* 1. to tint 2. to affect slightly
    n. a small amount of an added color or characteristic
    (v.1) The black soot in the air *tinged* her white blouse gray.
    (v.2) She worried that the unruly child would *tinge* the other students with a sense of defiance.
    (n) Adding a *tinge* of blue to the white walls would improve this room.
    (v.1) *syn: shade; color*
    (v.2) *syn: influence*
    (n) *syn: tint; shade*

14. **trivial** (triv´ ē əl) *adj.* of little importance
    After seeing what his friend endured, Ben felt that his own problems were *trivial*.
    syn: minor; insignificant   *ant: crucial; important*

15. **unkempt** (un kempt´) *adj.* maintained poorly; untidy
    The grass in the *unkempt* lawn stood two feet tall.
    syn: sloppy; messy   *ant: neat; trim*

EXERCISE I – Words in Context

Using the vocabulary list for this lesson, supply the correct word to complete each sentence.

1. Residents _____ the construction of a landfill less than a mile from their new homes.

2. The morning before the rainstorm was not the _____ time to wash a car.

3. The rusty metal will _____ the white gloves a shade of brown.

4. The _____ of the sentence was the word "not."

5. Miguel, who grew up in the country, dislikes the urban _____ of the city.

6. The damage to Brent's car seemed _____ when he thought about how lucky he was to have survived the accident.

7. Linda plans on retiring, but not before she chooses a[n] _____ to take her place.

8. Sylvia's _____ painting featured dead trees against a gray, winter sky.

9. The adult birds _____ the snake until it left the vicinity of the nest.

10. If you _____ your words, people will understand you.

11. Empty pizza boxes and old newspapers littered Tom's _____ apartment.

12. Please throw your _____ in the trash bin outside.

13. The _____ juror felt certain that the defendant was lying.

14. After the earthquake, rescue workers used dogs to find victims trapped beneath the _____.

15. After winning a Nobel Prize, the _____ scientist became an advisor to the president.

EXERCISE II – Sentence Completion

Complete the sentence in a way that shows you understand the meaning of the italicized vocabulary word.

1. Madeline determined that the *crux* of the matter is...

2. She thinks that 6:00 am is the *opportune* time to go jogging because...

3. The weeds growing in the lawn were a *trivial* problem until they...

4. The angry citizens *harassed* the corrupt mayor because...

5. The *articulate* student volunteered...

6. Someone who enjoys the oceanic *milieu* might decide to...

7. The loyal fan of the television series *decried* the network's decision to...

8. The white clothes will take on a red *tinge* if...

9. The bin overflowed with *refuse* because...

10. Robbie could not find anything in his *unkempt* locker because...

11. People cleaned up the *debris* after...

12. As she approached retirement age, she trained a *successor* who would...

13. We knew by her *sullen* expression that she...

14. Grandpa was always *skeptical* about...

15. The *eminent* scholar became famous when he...

EXERCISE III – Prefixes and Suffixes

Study the entries and use them to complete the questions that follow.

The prefix *in-* means "in" or "not."
The suffix *-ful* means "full of" or "having."
The suffix *-ion* means "act of," "state of," or "result."
The suffix *-ity* means "state of" or "quality of."

Use the provided prefixes and suffixes to change each word so that it completes the sentence correctly. Then, keeping in mind that prefixes and suffixes sometimes change the part of speech, identify the part of speech of the new word by circling N for a noun, V for a verb, or ADJ for an adjective.

1. (successor)   You need to practice every day if you want to have a[n]
    _____ career as a musician.   N   V   ADJ

2. (opportune)   When Caleb finally had a[n] _____ to see his
    favorite band live, a snowstorm caused the concert to be postponed.
                                             N   V   ADJ

3. (successor)   Students in the British History class had to memorize
    the _____ of English monarchs.   N   V   ADJ

4. (opportune)   The star player incurred a[n] _____ injury just
    hours before the championship game.   N   V   ADJ

EXERCISE IV – Critical Reading

The following reading passage contains vocabulary words from this lesson. Carefully read the passage and then choose the best answers for each of the questions that follow.

1   Upon hearing the name "Sherlock," many people instantly picture the world's most **eminent** fictional detective, complete with tweed, deerstalker cap, cape, magnifying glass, and pipe. A single glance at a footprint at the scene of the crime is all Sherlock Holmes needs to tell you the culprit's weight, occupation, and what injuries he or she might have sustained as a child. For more than a century, Mr. Holmes has amazed readers with his deductive ability; that is, his ability to infer facts from clues that other investigators dismiss as being **trivial** to the case. Sir Arthur Conan Doyle's creation would not have been complete, of course, without Sherlock's dependable sidekick, Doctor Watson, whose skills compensated for those forfeited by the great Holmes to make room for his matchless intellect. Together, Holmes and Watson have become icons of the mystery—the model for countless detective tales that feature a genius and a trusty sidekick working together to solve crimes; however, it is with no little surprise that many learn that Sherlock Holmes is but a mere **successor** to the original detective genius. Those who are **skeptical** of this need only read the adventures of C. Auguste Dupin—the first detective—in Edgar Allen Poe's "The Mystery of the Rue Morgue."

2   The first of three Dupin mysteries appeared in 1841, forty-six years before Sherlock Holmes debuted in the magazine serial *A Study in Scarlet*. Narrated by an unnamed sidekick, Poe's mysteries feature the extraordinary deductive abilities of the eccentric Auguste Dupin, an amateur detective in Paris. The brilliant Dupin uses his command of logic to reconstruct unsolvable crimes, twice at the request of police who overlook the clues at the **crux** of a mystery.

3   The Dupin mysteries establish several key elements that frequently appear in detective fiction. Dupin is the original deductive genius, a loner who relies upon his powers of logic and observation to decipher evidence. He trusts only his sidekick of lesser genius, and Dupin's sidekick, like Dr. Watson, is also the narrator of the story. Since Dupin corrects mistakes of police investigations, Poe's stories suggest a general lack of ability among police detectives. As a private detective, Sherlock Holmes also assists police who seemingly cannot perform their duties. Poe also introduces the concept of the wrongful accusation. In "The Mystery of the Rue Morgue," Dupin must solve a case to prove the innocence of a wrongfully accused friend—a popular plot for modern mystery and drama. Finally, Poe invented the "locked-room" mystery,

which involves setting a crime in a closed environment from which the criminal could not possibly escape, thus baffling investigators. Modern readers hear this technique humorously mocked each time someone exclaims, "The butler did it! In the den! With the bread knife!"

4   From the popularity of Sherlock Holmes extends a long line of fictional detective geniuses: Agatha Christie's Hercule Poirot and Miss Marple; Rex Stout's Nero Wolfe; Perry Mason; Charlie Chan; Simon Templar; Mike Hammer; and Sam Spade, to name a few. The detective mystery has spread from literature to television, and it is now nearly impossible to turn on a television without seeing at least two mysteries in progress that involve either private investigators or police detectives; however, whether you read mysteries or watch them, remember to thank Edgar Allen Poe, and his invention of Auguste Dupin, for making the mystery one of the most popular forms of entertainment.

1.   As used in paragraph 1, *eminent* most nearly means the opposite of
    A. weak.
    B. celebrated.
    C. popular.
    D. unknown.
    E. quiet.

2.   Sir Arthur Conan Doyle is
    A. the sidekick of the legendary Auguste Dupin.
    B. the author who created Sherlock Holmes.
    C. Auguste Dupin's unnamed narrator.
    D. the author who created Auguste Dupin.
    E. Dr. Watson's sidekick.

3.   As used in paragraph 2, *crux* most nearly means
    A. end.
    B. crime scene.
    C. heart.
    D. topic.
    E. evidence.

4.   According to paragraph 3, which is *not* an element of the detective story?
    A. deduction
    B. ghosts and supernatural events
    C. wrongful accusations
    D. inept police
    E. sidekick narrator

5.   Which of the following would be the *best* title for this passage?
     A.   Mystery Begins With Sherlock Holmes
     B.   Negative Portrayals of Police in Fiction
     C.   Literary Sidekicks
     D.   The Locked-Room Element in Modern Mystery
     E.   The Case of the Forgotten Detective

Lesson Two

1. **belittle**   (bi lit´ əl)   *v.*   to speak of someone or something as small or unimportant; to speak of negatively
    The arrogant professor sometimes *belittled* his students.
    syn: demean; criticize   *ant: praise; honor*

2. **blasé**   (blä zā´)   *adj.*   uninterested or unimpressed because of frequent exposure or excess
    Jillian's *blasé* attitude during the job interview convinced the manager to find a different applicant for the job.
    syn: unconcerned   *ant: enthusiastic*

3. **concoct**   (kən kokt´)   *v.*   to devise cleverly; to invent
    The writers *concocted* a new dilemma for the hero to overcome each week.
    syn: create; fabricate

4. **decade**   (dek´ ād)   *n.*   ten years
    Over the course of a *decade*, the tiny seed grew into a sizable tree.

5. **diverse**   (dī vûrs´)   *adj.*   differing from each other; many and distinctly unalike
    Adam has *diverse* tastes in music; he listens to everything from classical to hip-hop.
    syn: varied; assorted   *ant: homogeneous*

6. **enunciate**   (i nun´ sē āt)   *v.*   to speak articulately; to express clearly
    Please *enunciate* your words so the rest of the class can understand you.
                                                       ant: slur; mumble

7. **hurtle**   (hûr´ təl)   *v.*   1. to move with great speed and force
                                   2. to throw forcefully; to hurl
    (1) The runaway train *hurtled* down the tracks.
    (2) Kyle *hurtled* the dog's toy to the back of the yard.
    (1) *syn: race; bolt*   *ant: saunter; stroll*
    (2) *syn: heave; fling*

8. **improvise**   (im´ prə vīz)   *v.*   1. to do or make with no preparation
                                          2. to fashion using only immediately available materials
    (1) Dylan forgot the lyrics while he was on the stage, so he *improvised* the second half of the song.
    (2) The castaway *improvised* a crude raft out of barrels and rope.

9. **jostle** (jos´əl) *v.* to bump, push, or shove
Mark *jostled* the frozen log until it broke free from the ground.
syn: manhandle

10. **libel** (lī´bəl) *n.* the act of printing a false statement that harms
someone's reputation
v. to defame someone by publishing false statements
(n) The politician sued her opponent for *libel* after she read the obvious
lie printed in the advertisement.
(v) The newspaper refused to print the letter because it *libeled* a public
figure.
(n) *syn: defamation*   *ant: flattery*
(v) *syn: vilify*   *ant: praise; laud*

11. **mammoth** (mam´əth) *adj.* huge *n.* a large, hairy, extinct elephant
(adj) To promote business, the bakery made a *mammoth* 800-pound
cookie.
(n) The remains of the mammoth had been frozen in a glacier for
thousands of years.
(adj) *syn: enormous; immense*   *ant: tiny; petite*

12. **paradox** (pâr´ə doks) *n.* a statement or situation that is true, but
seems impossible or self-contradictory
To her friends, Dana's apparent ability to eat whatever she wants without
gaining any weight is a *paradox*.
syn: contradiction; impossibility

13. **provincial** (prə vin´shəl) *adj.* 1. rural; pertaining to the customs of
non-city dwellers 2. narrow in perspective; unsophisticated
(1) After eight years of working in the city, Phil missed his *provincial*
country home.
(2) His *provincial* argument failed to convince the principal to change her
mind.
(1) *syn: rustic*   *ant: urban*
(2) *syn: insular; unrefined*   *ant: broad-minded*

14. **realm** (relm) *n.* a domain; a field; a territory
The setting of the novel is a *realm* of fantasy, where elves and dragons
exist.
syn: world

15. **undermine** (un dər mīn´) *v.* to weaken by wearing away the
foundation or support
The sailor *undermined* the mission by turning the crew against the
captain.
syn: sabotage; destabilize   *ant: bolster; strengthen*

EXERCISE I – Words in Context

Using the vocabulary list for this lesson, supply the correct word to complete each sentence.

1.   Stranded and injured, Robinson used sticks and vines to _____ a sling for his broken arm.

2.   She is a good amateur golfer, but years will pass before she enters the _____ of professional golf.

3.   Uncle Pete _____ a disgusting beverage that he claimed would cure the common cold.

4.   The reporter lost his job after he _____ a respected judge in a newspaper article.

5.   Since Ed has _____ tastes, he is seldom seen trying any new foods.

6.   You must _____ your words if you want to be heard clearly.

7.   Everyone knew that the composer's career would soon be over when they saw the king's _____ expression during the concert.

8.   The _____ boulder tumbled down the mountain and smashed the sturdy, old cabin into pieces.

9.   The 1940s was a[n] _____ of war and invention.

10.   The statement, "this sentence is false," is a[n] _____ because it cannot be both true and false.

11.   Joe _____ the company by merely pretending to be working.

12.   The meteor _____ toward earth at ten times the speed of sound.

13.   The _____ team included people from various nations.

14.   On the morning after Thanksgiving, aggressive shoppers _____ each other while trying to be first to enter the department store.

15.   Many students _____ Donna's dedication to studying until she passed a test that everyone else failed.

EXERCISE II – Sentence Completion

Complete the sentence in a way that shows you understand the meaning of the italicized vocabulary word.

1.   Afraid that he would be punished if he told the truth, Martin *concocted*...

2.   Sam's *provincial* view of life is exemplified by...

3.   In the *realm* of her own dreams, Wanda is...

4.   The arrogant man *belittled* us because...

5.   It is a *paradox* that the company can lose money every year but still...

6.   The angry golfer *hurtled* his golf club into the pond after...

7.   The *blasé* film critic disliked the movie because...

8.   Eating *diverse* foods will ensure...

9.   She had to *improvise* her speech because...

10.   He *jostled* people in the crowd as he...

11.   She *enunciated* each word so...

12.   Johnny *undermines* the respect of his friends by...

13.   Over the course of a *decade*, the young maple sapling grew into...

14.   When the giant dropped his *mammoth* hat on the village, it caused...

15.   After being found guilty of *libel*, the reporter was ordered to...

EXERCISE III – Prefixes and Suffixes

Study the entries and use them to complete the questions that follow.

The suffix -*ify* means "to make."
The suffix -*ion* means "act of," "state of," or "result of."
The suffix -*ist* means "one who does" or "follower of."
The suffix -*ous* means "full of."

Use the provided prefixes and suffixes to change each word so that it completes the sentence correctly. Then, keeping in mind that prefixes and suffixes sometimes change the part of speech, identify the part of speech of the new word by circling N for a noun, V for a verb, or ADJ for an adjective.

1. (libel)   Though it was not truthful, the _____ article in the magazine ruined the actor's reputation.   N   V   ADJ

2. (diverse)   The stockbroker says clients should _____ their investments because it is risky to put all of one's savings in one place.
   N   V   ADJ

3. (libel)   The reporter earned a reputation as being a[n] _____ after he submitted a false story.   N   V   ADJ

4. (diverse)   The canoe trip was a nice _____ from an otherwise humdrum camping excursion.   N   V   ADJ

EXERCISE IV – Critical Reading

The following reading passage contains vocabulary words from this lesson.
Carefully read the passage and then choose the best answers for each of the ques-
tions that follow.

Stephanie Kwolek was born in 1923, in the small coal-mining town of New
Kensington, Pennsylvania, but her interests were anything but **provincial**.
Exploring the wilderness with her father filled Kwolek with a strong curiosity
of the natural world before she was ten years old. From her mother, Kwolek
5   learned to love sewing and working with fabrics. Some might call it a **paradox**
that Stephanie Kwolek, a woman who enjoyed nature and sewing as a young girl,
someday would devise a synthetic textile capable of stopping bullets.

Kwolek developed her interest in science and medicine, and after high school,
she enrolled in Margaret Morrison Carnegie College, the women's college of
10   what is now Carnegie Mellon University. She graduated in 1946 with a degree in
chemistry and applied for several jobs, one of which was a research position for
DuPont—a company already famous for its innovations in plastic and synthetic
fibers such as nylon.

Confidence and a little boldness landed Kwolek a job with the DuPont tex-
15   tile fiber laboratory in Buffalo, New York. Skill and determination allowed her
to retain her position in the years following the end of World War II, a time in
which many women scientists were **jostled** from their positions to make jobs for
returning male soldiers. During her first years at DuPont, Kwolek became very
interested in the **realm** of polymers, or chains of long molecules that make up
20   synthetic fibers. She abandoned her plans to go to medical school and focused on
her research at DuPont.

In 1950, Kwolek transferred to DuPont's new research laboratory in
Wilmington, Delaware. During the **decade** following the transfer, Kwolek labored
to identify new polymers and perfect low-temperature processes to create poly-
25   mers. Finally, in the 1960s, Kwolek discovered a phenomenon that resulted in a
whole new branch of the synthetic fiber industry: liquid crystal polymers (LCP).
The new polymers were merely the first part of a **mammoth** discovery. In 1965,
Kwolek prepared a cloudy, seemingly impure LCP solution with peculiar physical properties. She opted to spin the strange solution into fiber, but a reluctant
30   technician initially refused for fear of damaging the equipment. Kwolek insisted
on spinning the solution, and the results changed the world. The resultant fibers
were half the density of fiberglass but *five times stronger than their weight in steel.*
Kwolek had invented Kevlar®—the fiber now famous for its use in bulletproof
vests.

35   DuPont spent six years perfecting a commercial version of Kevlar, and
since entering the market in 1971, Kevlar has become the material of choice
for products that must be lightweight but durable enough to withstand physical
extremes. Kevlar is now found in hockey sticks, canoes, suspension bridge cables,
spacecraft shields, and hundreds of other products; however, its most celebrated
40   role is in that of lifesaving. Layers of Kevlar in body armor and protective clothing

protect thousands of police officers and soldiers from bullets, knife blades, and shrapnel each day.

45   Kwolek continued her research at DuPont until her semi-retirement in 1986. The discovery of Kevlar was a highlight of Kwolek's career, but it was certainly not the only one. Kwolek has received seventeen patents, and in 1994, she became the fourth woman in history to be inducted into the National Inventors Hall of Fame. In 1997, Kwolek became the second woman in a century to win the prestigious Perkins Medal for industrial chemistry. She has received the National Medal of

50   Technology, the Lemelson-MIT Lifetime Achievement Award, and, of course, the gratitude of the many whose lives were saved by Kwolek's discovery. Stephanie Kwolek is now an inspiration and mentor to scientists and students alike.

1.   Kwolek did not attend medical school because
    A.   medicine bored her.
    B.   she could not afford it.
    C.   only men could become doctors.
    D.   she worked at a hospital in Buffalo.
    E.   she enjoyed her job at DuPont.

2.   As used in line 17, the word *jostled* most nearly means
    A.   removed.
    B.   replaced.
    C.   empowered.
    D.   threatened.
    E.   promoted.

3.   Stephanie Kwolek invented
    A.   body armor made of nylon.
    B.   a type of synthetic fiber.
    C.   steel alloy used in textiles.
    D.   medical-grade nylon.
    E.   polymers.

4.   As used in line 27, *mammoth* most nearly means
    A.   widespread.
    B.   full-size.
    C.   major.
    D.   lifesaving.
    E.   inconsequential.

5.　This passage is best described as
   A.　biographical.
   B.　persuasive.
   C.　comical.
   D.　generous.
   E.　bleak.

Lesson Three

1. **amity** (am´ it ē) *n.* friendship
   In public, the siblings appeared to live in perfect *amity*, but behind closed doors, they fought incessantly.
   syn: peacefulness; harmony   *ant: disagreement; hostility*

2. **cater** (kāt´ ər) *v.* to supply what is needed or desired, especially support or food
   The restaurant *caters* to families by offering discounted children's meals.
   syn: provide; contribute   *ant: neglect; reject*

3. **guise** (gīz) *n.* a false appearance
   The waiter maintains a *guise* of friendliness with his customers in order to get a big tip.
   syn: semblance

4. **inconsequential** (in kon sə kwen´ shəl) *adj.* of little or no importance; irrelevant; without consequence
   The decision has been made, so any advice now will be *inconsequential*.
   syn: unnecessary; unrelated   *ant: appropriate; important*

5. **jubilant** (jōō´ bə lənt) *adj.* joyous, especially because of success
   The *jubilant* student smiled all day after getting a perfect score on her lengthy term paper.
   syn: elated; happy   *ant: depressed; disappointed*

6. **placate** (plā´ kāt) *v.* to calm; to pacify
   The manager tried to *placate* the angry customer by reducing the bill.
   syn: appease; satisfy   *ant: enrage; anger*

7. **preclude** (pri klōōd´) *v.* to prevent
   Having a criminal record *precludes* a teaching career.
   syn: prohibit; forbid   *ant: allow; permit*

8. **repress** (ri pres´) *v.* to hold back or put down with force; to suppress
   The dictator *represses* dissenters with threats of imprisonment.
   syn: restrain; stifle   *ant: release; permit*

9. **saturate** (sach´ ə rāt) *v.* to fill or soak to capacity
   The heavy rains *saturated* the soil.
   syn: drench; permeate; infuse   *ant: desiccate; sear; parch*

10. **slake** (slāk) *v.* 1. to satisfy; to quench 2. to make less intense
    (1) The exhausted worker *slaked* his thirst by downing two glasses of lemonade.
    (2) Seeing someone else make the same mistake *slaked* his embarrassment.
    (1) *syn: fulfill; please*
    (2) *syn: abate; mitigate; diminish*   *ant: intensify; amplify*

11. **sortie** (sôr´ tē) *n.* 1. a flight of a combat aircraft on a mission
               2. an armed attack, especially against surrounding enemy forces
    (1) The fighter jet was riddled with bullet holes after the *sortie*.
    (2) The colonel ordered an immediate *sortie* to stall the enemy's offensive.
    (2) *syn: maneuver; assault*

12. **succumb** (sə kum´) *v.* to submit reluctantly; to yield
    After weeks of constant bombing, the enemy finally *succumbed* to our overwhelming force.
    syn: give in; surrender   *ant: withstand; resist*

13. **tranquil** (trang´ kwəl) *adj.* calm; peaceful
    Lonnie looked forward to a *tranquil* day of gardening in the back yard.
    syn: placid; serene   *ant: bustling; busy*

14. **venomous** (ven´ ə məs) *adj.* 1. poisonous
               2. intentionally harmful; malevolent
    (1) Go to the hospital if that *venomous* spider bites you.
    (2) His *venomous* remarks shocked everyone in the room.
    (1) *syn: toxic; noxious; lethal*   *ant: harmless; innocuous; safe*
    (2) *syn: malicious; spiteful; cruel*   *ant: benevolent; benign; kind*

15. **wrest** (rest´) *v.* to obtain through force, usually by twisting and turning violently
    Citizens *wrested* the dagger from the madman on the subway.
    syn: wring; wrench

EXERCISE I – Words in Context

Using the vocabulary list for this lesson, supply the correct word to complete each sentence.

1. On the night before the siege, the defenders launched eight _____ against the invaders.

2. The mouse _____ the angry lion by removing a thorn from his paw.

3. He started a[n] _____ rumor meant to ruin his rival's reputation.

4. The minor scratches were _____ to the value of the priceless artifact.

5. Some people _____ their bad memories until they have emotional breakdowns.

6. The surgeon _____ the sterile cloth with alcohol before using it to clean the patient's wound.

7. The _____ team held a banquet to celebrate its winning season.

8. The people in the lifeboat had no water, but they did not dare _____ their thirst with seawater.

9. If Thomas _____ to exhaustion and stops walking, he may never make it out of the desert.

10. When the looter _____ the pouch of gold from the skeleton's hand, he triggered a booby trap that fired poison darts at him.

11. The two rivals used to argue all the time, but now _____ exists between them.

12. The _____ setting of the cabin provided the peace and quiet necessary to write a novel.

13. During the cruise, waiters _____ to the needs of every passenger.

14. An unexpected, drenching rainstorm _____ the long-awaited victory.

15. Using the _____ of a pizza-delivery man, the undercover detective infiltrated the criminal's hideout.

EXERCISE II – Sentence Completion

Complete the sentence in a way that shows you understand the meaning of the italicized vocabulary word.

1. Rachael had to *placate* her son when...

2. During the *sortie*, two soldiers...

3. To *slake* his day-to-day frustrations, Alex likes to...

4. The *jubilant* townspeople hosted a festival to...

5. A flat tire *precluded* our plan to...

6. Be sure to *saturate* the sponge before...

7. Mia's *tranquil* afternoon was ruined when...

8. If you practice self-discipline, you will not *succumb* to...

9. The new store near the industrial park plans to *cater* to...

10. Kayla disrupted the *amity* within her neighborhood when she...

11. The thief tried to *wrest*...

12. Her *venomous* attitude spread among the other workers until...

13. The king *repressed* any subjects who...

14. Austin struggled to put on a *guise* of gratefulness when his aunt gave him...

15. The effort you put into your essay will be *inconsequential* if you...

EXERCISE III – Prefixes and Suffixes

Study the entries and use them to complete the questions that follow.

The suffix *-ize* means "to become" or "to cause to become."
The suffix *-ity* means "state of" or "quality of."
The suffix *-able* means "able to be."
The suffix *-ion* means "act of," "state of," or "result of."

Use the provided prefixes and suffixes to change each word so that it completes the sentence correctly. Then, keeping in mind that prefixes and suffixes sometimes change the part of speech, identify the part of speech of the new word by circling N for a noun, V for a verb, or ADJ for an adjective.

1. (placate) The mere sound of a soothing voice caused the _____ infant to stop crying and fall asleep.   N   V   ADJ

2. (tranquil) The wildlife official must _____ the elephant before he can attach a tracking device to the animal's ear.

    N   V   ADJ

3. (placate) After an enormous scandal in the city government, years of _____ were necessary before citizens again trusted elected officials.

    N   V   ADJ

4. (tranquil) The _____ of the snowy landscape was lost when a train rumbled through the center of the field.

    N   V   ADJ

EXERCISE IV – Improving Paragraphs

Read the following passage and then answer the multiple-choice questions that follow. The questions will require you to make decisions regarding the revision of the reading selection.

1 In May of 2002, construction workers on a routine job uncovered something far from **inconsequential**: the tomb of a man who died in 2400 BC—the early Bronze Age. Anthropologists were summoned to the town of Amesbury, Wiltshire, United Kingdom, to examine the discovery made just two miles from the famous Stonehenge monument.

2 The objects found in the tomb raised many questions. During this period of the Bronze Age, only the most respected and powerful citizens received extravagant burial rites; most bodies were simply dumped into a river. Who was this archer, in such an elaborate tomb? Why was he missing part of his leg?

3 The scientists immediately noted several things about the man in the tomb. He had been buried with a hunter's knife and arrows, and he was apparently rich, at least by the standards of the day, because he had been buried with a number of gold artifacts—the oldest ever found in Britain. Also, curiously, the kneecap of the man was not with him.

4 Examination of the skeleton revealed that the man did not **succumb** to the substantial wound on his leg; the injury occurred long before the man's death. He must have been in excellent physical condition at the time he was wounded.

5 Tests on the gold revealed that it came not from the British Isles but from a region near Switzerland. Dwellers of Bronze-Age Britain were known to have contact with mainland Europe, but the discovery of the archer—an ancient foreigner—suggests **amity** existed between the Isles and the continent.

6 Examiners also found a *cushion stone* in the tomb, which is a small stone used to sharpen metalworking tools. Was the man a metalworker in the **guise** of a hunter? The evidence did not **preclude** either of these things.

7 The man, now called the "Amesbury Archer," is still shrouded in mystery. He came from outside Britain, and he brought with him the beginnings of the metalworking trade. He was a part of the community, and respected enough to receive a funeral with honors. In time, studying the archer will bring us a step closer to understanding how, more than 4,000 years ago, civilization began in England.

1. Paragraph 2 should be moved to follow
    A. paragraph 1 (no change).
    B. paragraph 3.
    C. paragraph 4.
    D. paragraph 5.
    E. paragraph 6.

2. Which revision best clarifies the underlined portion of this sentence from paragraph 3?

    Also, curiously, <u>the kneecap of the man was not with him.</u>

    A. the man's missing kneecap was not there.
    B. someone had stolen the man's kneecap.
    C. the man's kneecap was missing.
    D. the kneecap was also made of gold.
    E. the man had no kneecaps.

3. Adding which sentence would help to clarify paragraph 4?
    A. The man was probably accustomed to being wounded because he was an archer.
    B. Apparently, the man's wealth kept him supplied with primitive medicine.
    C. The wound was most likely the result of an enemy's arrow on the battlefield.
    D. The man probably suffered great pain each day of his life; such a wound in the Bronze Age might prove lethal to most people.
    E. During the Bronze Age, people learned to combine copper and tin to make bronze, and bronze weapons inflicted deep wounds.

4. Which sentence best describes the importance of the Amesbury Archer to the world?
    A. In time, studying the archer will bring us a step closer to under-standing how, more than 4,000 years ago, civilization began in England.
    B. During this period of the Bronze Age, only the most respected and powerful citizens warranted extravagant burial rites; most bodies were simply dumped into a river.
    C. The man, now called the "Amesbury Archer," is still shrouded in mystery.
    D. Dwellers of Bronze-Age Britain were known to have contact with mainland Europe, but the discovery of the archer—an ancient foreigner—suggests **amity** existed between the Isles and the conti-nent.
    E. Who was this archer, in such an elaborate tomb?

Review

Lessons 1 – 3

EXERCISE I – Inferences

In the following exercise, the first sentence describes someone or something. Infer information from the first sentence, and then choose the word from the Word Bank that best completes the second sentence.

Word Bank

sullen	opportune	articulate	skeptical
diverse	blasé	jubilant	venomous

1. With few words, Lucinda clearly made her point, leaving no one with doubt and uncertainty.
    From this sentence, we can infer that Lucinda is _____.

2. Whenever we presented Jefferson with new revelations, he required lengthy explanations and a great deal of evidence before he would accept any new information as truth.
    From this sentence, we can infer that Jefferson is _____.

3. Janice eagerly seized the opportunity every time the group offered her a new assignment.
    From this sentence, we can infer that Janice is the opposite of _____.

4. The entire class anticipated Mr. Anderson's visits, for he always managed to instill them with renewed enthusiasm and willingness to put forth their best efforts.
    From this sentence, we can infer that Mr. Anderson is _____.

5. Feeling hurt and discouraged by Antoinette's remarks, Joyce secluded herself in her room for the rest of the day.
    From this sentence, we can infer that Antoinette's remarks were _____.

EXERCISE II – Related Words

Some of the vocabulary words from lessons 1–3 have related meanings. Complete the following sentences by choosing the word that best completes the specified relationship. Some word pairs will be antonyms, some will be synonyms, and some will be words often used in the same context.

1. *Articulate* most nearly means
    A. harass.
    B. libel.
    C. undermine.
    D. enunciate.
    E. tinge.

2. The word that best contrasts with *undermine* is
    A. cater.
    B. wrest.
    C. hurtle.
    D. refuse.
    E. concoct.

3. The word that most nearly means *refuse* is
    A. amity.
    B. milieu.
    C. crux.
    D. debris.
    E. sortie.

4. *Jubilant* is nearly the opposite of
    A. tranquil.
    B. provincial.
    C. trivial.
    D. eminent.
    E. sullen.

5. The best substitute for the word *milieu* is
    A. guise.
    B. realm.
    C. paradox.
    D. sortie.
    E. blasé.

6. If something is *inconsequential*, then it is probably
   A. trivial.
   B. opportune.
   C. articulate.
   D. venomous.
   E. jubilant.

7. The word most synonymous with *improvise* is
   A. undermine.
   B. refuse.
   C. libel.
   D. repress.
   E. concoct.

8. A *provincial* course of study would not rely upon _____ sources of knowledge.
   A. unkempt
   B. diverse
   C. eminent
   D. tranquil
   E. sullen

9. *Slake* most nearly means
   A. repress.
   B. concoct.
   C. undermine.
   D. placate.
   E. tinge.

10. A dictator might *repress* citizens until they _____ to his or her rule.
    A. jostle
    B. saturate
    C. succumb
    D. wrest
    E. articulate

EXERCISE III – Crossword Puzzle

Use the clues to complete the crossword puzzle. The answers consist of vocabulary words from lessons 1 through 3.

Across

3. The huge catapult will _____ boulders at the castle walls.
5. Traveling back in time and kidnapping yourself would create a[n] _____.
6. The retired principal's _____ changed many of the school programs.
7. The _____ teacher did not believe the student's excuse for being late.
10. After a few months in the busy city, Sharon missed the _____ atmosphere of the country.
12. It is not wise to _____ others, for you may soon find that you are not truly better than everyone else.
13. The space ranger tried to _____ the photon pistol from the hand of the villain.
14. She is _____ about going to the movie because she has seen it already.

Down

1. The man at the flea market sold fake designer sunglasses under the _____ that they were genuine.
2. In her letter to the newspaper, she plans to _____ the town's mayor for his involvement in a scandal.
4. Forget about the unimportant matters and get to the _____ of the problem.
5. The player's knee injury will _____ his sports career.
8. The _____ scholar receives requests to speak at schools throughout the nation.
9. Jenna had to _____ people to get off the crowded subway train.
11. The nations lived in _____ until the war made everyone enemies.

Lesson Four

1. **acute** (ə kyōōt´) *adj.* serious and sudden
    Boris contracted an *acute* case of food poisoning, which landed him in the hospital.
    syn: severe; critical   *ant: minor*

2. **durable** (door´ ə bəl) *adj.* able to withstand wear, decay, or certain tough conditions; long-lasting
    The hiker bought *durable* boots that would not fall apart on the trail.
    syn: sturdy; dependable   *ant: fragile; shoddy*

3. **eavesdrop** (ēvz´ drop) *v.* to listen secretly to private conversations
    Mike put his ear against the door and *eavesdropped* on the parent-teacher conference.
    syn: overhear; snoop   *ant: ignore; avoid*

4. **ethical** (eth´ ik əl) *adj.* 1. pertaining to accepted standards of behavior
    2. conforming to accepted standards of behavior
    (1) Whether doctors should be allowed to date patients is an *ethical* matter.
    (2) It is not *ethical* for judges to accept bribes.
    (1) *syn: moral*
    (2) *syn: virtuous; decent; moral*   *ant: corrupt; dishonest*

5. **fjord** (fyôrd) *n.* a narrow inlet of the sea between tall cliffs or steep banks
    The pirates sailed into a *fjord* to hide from the Royal Navy.

6. **gaudy** (gô´ dē) *adj.* tastelessly showy
    The walls of Andrea's *gaudy* living room were covered with mismatched, brightly colored pictures, objects, and knickknacks.
    syn: flashy; extravagant   *ant: tasteful; elegant*

7. **nominal** (nom´ ə nəl) *adj.* 1. existing in name only
    2. insignificantly small; token
    (1) The *nominal* change to the rules pleased critics, but other than restating what was already written, the change did nothing to the original document.
    (2) The non-profit charity writes letters asking for *nominal* donations.
    (1) *syn: supposed*   *ant: genuine; authentic*
    (2) *syn: minimal; trivial*   *ant: momentous; vast*

8. **nurture** (nûr´ chûr) *v.* to nourish; to help grow or develop
Elizabeth *nurtured* the injured bird until it could fly again.
syn: foster; raise   *ant: neglect; hinder*

9. **pommel** (pom´ məl) *v.* to strike; to beat   *n.* a knob on the handle of a sword or weapon
(v) The heavyweight boxers *pommeled* one another with their meaty fists until neither man was recognizable.
(n) The knight struck the ogre with the *pommel* of his sword.
(v) *syn: batter; pound*

10. **quibble** (kwib´ əl) *v.* to evade the main point by arguing over petty details   *n.* an irrelevant argument
(v) Darlene knew that she had been caught, but when confronted about her crime, she *quibbled* in order to delay punishment.
(n) Except for one or two minor *quibbles*, there was no opposition to the proposed bill.
(v) *syn: equivocate; hedge*   *ant: acknowledge; admit*

11. **rampart** (ram´ pərt) *n.* a defensive structure or embankment
In the safety of the *ramparts*, troops prepared for the final attack.
syn: bulwark; fortification; battlement

12. **respite** (res´ pit) *n.* a short rest or period of relief; delay
The surgeon toiled without *respite* through the first night of the battle.
syn: break; lull; recess

13. **rite** (rīt) *n.* a customary or religious ceremonial act
As a *rite* of passage to enter adulthood, the young men in the tribe must survive in the wilderness for one full month.
syn: ritual; custom

14. **seismic** (sīz´ mik) *adj.* pertaining to earthquakes or vibrations of the earth
The mildest *seismic* disturbance could topple the condemned building.

15. **terrestrial** (tə res´ trē əl) *adj.* of or pertaining to solid land
Captain Nemo gave up his *terrestrial* existence to live at sea.
syn: earthly   *ant: extraterrestrial; heavenly*

EXERCISE I – Words in Context

Using the vocabulary list for this lesson, supply the correct word to complete each sentence.

1. The world's largest _____ animal, the elephant, is small compared to the largest aquatic animal, the blue whale.

2. Johnny found it easier to accept responsibility for the accident than to _____ over who was responsible.

3. He draped the dusty rug over a clothesline and _____ it with a stick until no more dust fell out of it.

4. The entry fee is _____, especially for such a once-in-a-lifetime event.

5. On the general's order, thousands of troops charged the _____ surrounding the city.

6. Geologists noticed an increase in _____ activity from the volcano.

7. Space vehicles must be _____ enough to withstand extreme forces and temperatures.

8. The Vikings used long poles to push their ship away from the craggy walls of the _____.

9. Carlos _____ on conversations when he thinks someone might be talking about him.

10. A short _____ in the afternoon gave the workers enough energy to finish the job.

11. The art class is meant to _____ the talents of young artists.

12. In some cultures, teenagers must participate in _____ that mark their passage into adulthood.

13. The famous pianist wore a[n] _____ coat covered with rhinestones, sequins, and fur.

14. A[n] _____ illness caused Leonid to miss his concert.

15. Psychologists who fail to practice _____ conduct will lose their licenses.

EXERCISE II – Sentence Completion

Complete the sentence in a way that shows you understand the meaning of the italicized vocabulary word.

1. From behind the *ramparts*, soldiers watched...

2. An octopus is not a *terrestrial* animal because...

3. After observing increased *seismic* activity, scientists...

4. As a *rite* of membership, each person in the club must...

5. After a short *respite*, the workers are expected to...

6. Ron had *nurtured* the plant for years, so he was angry when...

7. The grizzly bear *pommeled* the flopping salmon until...

8. The *nominal* promotion gave her a better job title, but...

9. Nathan *eavesdropped* on his parents because he wanted to know...

10. She likes *gaudy* fashion accessories such as...

11. Navigating the *fjord* is hazardous because...

12. It is not *ethical* for a judge to...

13. She bought *durable* furniture that would...

14. The devastating hurricane created an *acute* need for...

15. The defendant *quibbled* when the judge asked...

EXERCISE III – Prefixes and Suffixes

Study the entries and use them to complete the questions that follow.

The prefix *en-* means "into" or "against."
The suffix *-ation* means "act of" or "result of."
The suffix *-graph* means "writing."
The suffix *-logy* or *-ology* means "science of."

Use the provided prefixes and suffixes to change each word so that it completes the sentence correctly. Then, keeping in mind that prefixes and suffixes sometimes change the part of speech, identify the part of speech of the new word by circling N for a noun, V for a verb, or ADJ for an adjective.

1. (seismic) A person interested in earthquakes might decide to study
   _____.   N   V   ADJ

2. (durable) Members of the audience were asked to turn off their cell
   phones for the _____ of the movie.
                                              N   V   ADJ

3. (seismic) The _____ detected vibrations of the earth and depicted
   them as sweeping lines on paper.
                                              N   V   ADJ

4. (durable) The stranded hikers must _____ the harsh weather until
   the rescue helicopter finds them.
                                              N   V   ADJ

EXERCISE IV – Critical Reading

The following reading passage contains vocabulary words from this lesson. Carefully read the passage and then choose the best answers for each of the questions that follow.

1   Lieutenant Frank Luke, the young, overconfident aviator, could not seem to please anyone at the 27ᵗʰ Aero Squadron. Assigned to an airfield near the Allied front in July of 1918, Luke alienated himself from the veteran pilots by boasting about his unproven skills and by routinely abandoning his formation to fly off on his own. So scornful of Luke were the other pilots that no one believed him when he, without witness, shot down a German plane during a patrol. Branded a braggart and a liar, the 21-year-old aviator from Arizona withdrew to outsider status.

2   Luke spent his free hours honing his marksmanship, fine-tuning his problematic Spad-13, and thinking of ways to prove himself. He found one when he heard pilots talking about German observation balloons, or *Drachen*. Quietly, Luke committed himself to a task that would secure him a place in history.

3   Observers in balloons hovering high above the German **ramparts** directed artillery fire with deadly accuracy. Shells **pommeled** Allied positions, forcing soldiers to take cover in the muddy, disease-ridden trenches. Expensive to build and crucial to battlefield advantage, the balloons were heavily defended by anti-aircraft cannons and squadrons of German fighter planes. The Allies needed to destroy the balloons, but pilots knew that such missions were suicide; a defensive wall of *archie*, or anti-aircraft fire, shredded any plane that approached a Drachen. Even if a pilot were lucky enough to set fire to a balloon, he risked going down with it when the balloon's gas exploded into a massive fireball. Only a maniac would volunteer for such a mission; a maniac, that is, or Frank Luke.

4   The American offensive began on the morning of September 12, 1918, and Luke's squadron took to the skies with orders to protect Allied balloons. Despite the orders, most of the pilots flew straight for the German line. In his typical **rite**, Luke separated from his squadron and flew well beyond his designated zone. He soon spotted the opportunity he was waiting for: a Drachen suspended above the horizon.

5   Luke pulled back on the stick and forced his Spad to climb high above the balloon. Luke closed the distance, and then the Spad's engine raced as Luke shoved the control stick to the firewall and plunged toward the Drachen. Shells burst around the Spad, the shrapnel tearing through its canvas wings and wood frame. Explosions surrounded Luke, but he grunted through them, accelerating, until he was on a collision course with the balloon. The Spad's twin machine guns opened up, their clacking

inaudible amid the wind and bursting shells. At the last moment, Luke pulled up—the balloon was intact. Determined, even as his plane was slowly being shot to pieces, Luke made a second pass, holding the trigger until his guns jammed. The balloon remained, and the archie became more intense. Running out of time, Luke beat his jammed guns with a hammer as he lined up for a third pass. The guns barked to life, and almost inst- antly, the balloon erupted into a great firestorm of burning gas, nearly taking the Spad with it.

6   Wires, shredded wood, and ragged canvas dangled from the edges of Luke's plane when he landed it behind the Allied trenches, short of the airfield. Allied soldiers ran to the shot-up plane, thrilled by the spectacle they had just seen in the sky. Luke, worried that no one would believe him again, collected witness statements from the infantrymen.

7   Luke's first balloon-busting mission did not win him friends, but it did gain him credit as a combat pilot and two more weeks of intense balloon-attack missions, many of which were more harrowing than the first. In seventeen days, Luke went on to destroy thirteen more balloons and four enemy planes, making him the second highest-scoring American ace of World War I. Historians still **quibble** about Luke's first unconfirmed victory, but its relevance is overshadowed by Luke's sacrifice.

8   Lieutenant Luke met his fate shortly after he flamed an unbelievable three balloons in fifteen minutes. Ground fire and eight German fighter planes had severely damaged Luke's Spad, but before Luke was forced to land in enemy territory, he fired upon a German infantry column. Luke survived the landing, but the soldiers soon caught up with him. He died fighting his would-be captors. Frank Luke's name is now memorialized by Luke Air Force Base in Arizona.

1.   Germans protected the Drachen because
    A. balloons weakened the morale of Allied troops.
    B. balloons were cheap and effective.
    C. artillery was useless without spotters in balloons.
    D. balloons were the first line of German defense.
    E. balloons were costly and allowed precise attacks on the enemy.

2.   As used in paragraph 3, *pommeled* most nearly means the opposite of
    A. battered.
    B. cleaned.
    C. hit.
    D. helped.
    E. freed.

3.   *Archie* is
     A.   the name of Frank Luke's only friend in the squadron.
     B.   a nickname for anti-aircraft fire.
     C.   the nickname for Frank Luke.
     D.   Frank Luke's squadron commander.
     E.   a nickname for the German observation balloons.

4.   As used in paragraph 4, *rite* most nearly means
     A.   defiance.
     B.   habit.
     C.   bravery.
     D.   stubbornness.
     E.   assignment.

5.   Which choice best describes the *purpose* of paragraphs 1 and 2?
     A.   They explain factors that motivated Luke's daring attacks.
     B.   They prove that Luke was unfit to be a pilot.
     C.   They suggest Luke's fear of heights.
     D.   They explain the reasons for World War I.
     E.   They portray Frank Luke as an unlikable person.

Lesson Five

1. **bizarre** (bi zär´) *adj.* extremely unusual; strange
   The *bizarre* behavior of the animals signaled that something was wrong.
   syn: unusual; weird   *ant: ordinary; normal*

2. **bungle** (bung´ gəl) *v.* to act or work clumsily; to ruin something
   through clumsiness
   Kevin was fired after he *bungled* a job and lost a valuable client.
   syn: botch   *ant: manage; succeed*

3. **deduce** (di dōōs´) *v.* to conclude by reasoning; to infer
   After examining the clues at the crime scene, the detective *deduced* that
   the death was accidental.
   syn: determine; understand   *ant: misconstrue; mistake*

4. **dynamic** (dī nam´ ik) *adj.*   1. energetic; intense; forceful
                                     2. continuously active or changing
   (1) The *dynamic* speaker at the school assembly captured everyone's
       attention.
   (2) Land in the Midwest might be flat, but the region has some of the
       most *dynamic* weather patterns in the world.
   (1) *syn: powerful; active*   *ant: mild; calm; lifeless*

5. **irrelevant** (i rel´ ə vənt) *adj.* unimportant to the matter at hand
   Carol thought geometry was *irrelevant* to her life until she had to calcu-
   late the area of her lawn.
   syn: inapplicable; immaterial   *ant: pertinent; germane*

6. **loiter** (loi´ tər) *v.* to linger without an apparent purpose
   Some of the teenagers do nothing but *loiter* in front of the arcade.
   syn: dawdle; amble   *ant: hurry; hasten*

7. **obstinate** (ob´ stə nit) *adj.* stubborn
   It took ten minutes for the farmer to get the *obstinate* cow across the
   road.
   syn: headstrong   *ant: obedient; compliant*

8. **scrutinize** (skrōōt´ n īz) *v.* to examine in great detail
   The board *scrutinized* the record of each applicant before choosing one to
   receive the scholarship.
   syn: study; inspect   *ant: skim; browse*

9. **stunt**   (stunt)   *v.* to limit or hinder growth
                            n. an unusual or dangerous feat
   (v) The drought *stunted* the growth of the crops.
   (n) The television reporter participated in a *stunt* designed to increase ratings.
   (v) *syn: inhibit*   *ant: nurture*

10. **superficial** (sōō pər fish´ əl) *adj.* 1. on or near the surface
                              2. concerned with the obvious only; shallow   3. insignificant; trivial
   (1) His *superficial* wounds did not require immediate medical attention.
   (2) The *superficial* man at the party could quote many texts, but understood few.
   (3) She gets angry when *superficial* matters interfere with the completion of the mission.
   (1) *syn: external*   *ant: inner; deep*
   (2) *syn: depthless; perfunctory*   *ant: sincere; deep; profound*
   (3) *syn: unimportant; trifling*   *ant: important; crucial*

11. **ultimate** (ul´ tə mit) *adj.* 1. last in a series; conclusive; final
                              2. highest; extreme
   (1) The boss will make the *ultimate* decision as to who gets hired.
   (2) Gary thought that he had written the *ultimate* novel until he received a dozen rejection letters from publishers.
   (1) *syn: terminal*   *ant: original; earliest*
   (2) *syn: supreme; greatest*   *ant: worst; lowest; slightest*

12. **vapid** (vap´ id) *adj.* bland; dull
   The food critic claimed that the *vapid* main course required additional spices.
   syn: uninteresting; unexciting   *ant: zesty*

13. **viable** (vī´ ə bəl) *adj.* capable of succeeding, working, or living
   The escape plan may sound crazy, but it is definitely *viable*.
   syn: feasible; possible   *ant: impossible; hopeless*

14. **wan** (won) *adj.* unnaturally pale, as from illness or distress
   Dora had a *wan* complexion after narrowly avoiding an accident.
   syn: pallid; pasty   *ant: flushed; ruddy*

15. **wane** (wān) *v.* to decrease gradually
   The moon *wanes* after a full moon.
   (v) *syn: diminish; decline; recede*   *ant: wax; grow; enlarge*

EXERCISE I – Words in Context

Using the vocabulary list for this lesson, supply the correct word to complete each sentence.

1. The club will not survive if interest continues to _____.

2. The towering maple tree _____ the younger trees by blocking the sunlight.

3. The committee created a[n] _____ plan to reduce homelessness in the city once and for all.

4. The new book was criticized as a[n] _____ biography of an equally unexciting person.

5. Your grade is based entirely on your writing; the type of paper you use is _____.

6. Having been seasick for hours, the passenger looked _____ in the face and weak in the knees.

7. The store owners do not want people to _____ in front of the entrance because they block the entry of potential customers.

8. Hector _____ his photography project when he accidentally exposed all the film.

9. Historians _____ the ancient document to be certain that it was authentic.

10. Everyone said he was wasting his time, but the _____ prospector kept digging until he eventually struck gold.

11. Gina has the _____ belief that physical appearance is more important than character.

12. The _____ growth of the region requires that the map be revised every two years.

13. From the performance of the team, the coach _____ that it would have a winning season.

14. Visiting the petting zoo is the _____ experience for children who love animals.

15. The astrologer believed that the meteor shower's occurring during the eclipse was more than just some _____ coincidence.

EXERCISE II – Sentence Completion

Complete the sentence in a way that shows you understand the meaning of the italicized vocabulary word.

1. Mitch could have gotten away with the crime, but he made the *ultimate* decision to...

2. To persuade her *obstinate* son to go to the dentist, Gayle...

3. The *wan* color of her face indicated...

4. Irene wants a *dynamic* career in which...

5. Chad must give his parents one *viable* reason for wanting to...

6. If you *loiter* in front of the bank too long, people might think...

7. For a publicity *stunt*, Carl decided to...

8. The most *bizarre* item in Tim's collection is...

9. His parents *scrutinized* his report card because...

10. Jill thinks the old music is *vapid*, but her parents...

11. Tosha felt her feelings were *irrelevant* in the matter because...

12. He had only a *superficial* understanding of the subject until he...

13. If Pat *bungles* the science project, he...

14. You should allow your anger to *wane* before...

15. After investigating the remnants of the burned-out building, the fire marshal *deduced*...

EXERCISE III – Prefixes and Suffixes

Study the entries and use them to complete the questions that follow.

The suffix *-able* means "able to be."
The suffix *-ance* means "state of" or "quality of."
The suffix *-er* means "one who does."
The suffix *-y* means "condition of" or "quality of."

Use the provided prefixes and suffixes to change each word so that it completes the sentence correctly. Then, keeping in mind that prefixes and suffixes sometimes change the part of speech, identify the part of speech of the new word by circling N for a noun, V for a verb, or ADJ for an adjective.

1. (irrelevant) Because of the _____ of her question, everyone could tell that she had not completed the reading assignment.

             N V ADJ

2. (scrutinize) His essay will be published if it withstands the _____ of the magazine's editor. N V ADJ

3. (bungle) The mistakes of a single _____ who works on the assembly line ruined an entire shipment of the factory's product.

             N V ADJ

4. (scrutinize) The stone tablets are _____ to anyone who happens to know how to read ancient Sumerian. N V ADJ

EXERCISE IV – Critical Reading

The following reading passage contains vocabulary words from this lesson. Carefully read the passage and then choose the best answers for each of the questions that follow.

In September of 1961, one of the most **bizarre** events in the history of the paranormal occurred in the White Mountains of New Hampshire. Driving home from a visit to Canada, Barney and Betty Hill noticed a strange light in the sky. Before the end of the night, Betty and Barney
5   would become the first couple in history to have reported the phenomenon now known as an "alien abduction."

The light grew more intense as the Hills approached the White Mountains, but the couple dismissed it as a helicopter or low-flying plane. The light darted from side to side with amazing quickness, and
10   it seemed to come closer with each movement. It was not until the light slowed and **loitered** above the road ahead that Barney and Betty became worried. Taking his binoculars, Barney stepped out of the car and peered at the light, now only a hundred feet away. He later described it as "banana-like with pointed tips and windows." Barney walked closer,
15   resisting the fear that was rapidly overwhelming him. Barney saw what appeared to be figures moving behind the windows, as many as eleven. Terrified, Barney suddenly became aware of Betty, screaming for him to return to the car. The Hills wasted no time as they motored down the highway, but the light followed, growing larger as the Hills retreated.
20   When the strange craft was directly over the car, the Hill's heard a strange noise, like that of a tuning fork. What happened to the Hills next would perplex them for the rest of their lives.

Stunned and feeling strange, the Hills awoke, in their car, thirty-five miles from where they had stopped to observe the light. Bewildered and
25   insecure, they drove home.

The next day, Betty called nearby Pease Air Force Base to report the incident. The base told Betty that something unidentified had indeed been detected near the exact spot where she and Barney had stopped; however, there was no **viable** proof or explanation of what had happened, so the
30   Hills moved on with their lives. Barney simply tried to forget about the night, but Betty could not put the event behind her quite so easily.

Nightmares plagued Betty in the nights following the abduction. In the dreams, a group of men took Betty and Barney aboard a craft and conducted medical tests on the couple. Beleaguered by the nightmares, and
35   increasingly aware of the strangeness of the evening, the Hills sought help from a psychiatrist who used hypnosis to treat amnesia. In a short time, the Hills realized that two hours had elapsed on that September night

for which they had no recollection. For the next six months, the Hills struggled to piece together the lost time. Under hypnosis, Barney sketched
40   the creatures he claimed to have seen: short beings with pale faces, large heads, and enormous, cat-like eyes—what has since become the common description of so many aliens in books and television. Betty's descriptions matched those of Barney's, and she even sketched a "star map" that the aliens allegedly showed her during the abduction. Some have found the
45   map to be a curiously accurate depiction of *Zeta Reticuli*, a twin star system not fully mapped until 1969.

     Experts have **scrutinized** the Hills' story, authors have written about it, and it has even been portrayed on film, but no one has been able to **deduce** what really happened on that September night. The Hills' psychia-
50   trist suggested that the episode was a product of imagination, emphasizing that people under hypnosis tell what they *believe* to be the truth—not necessarily the *factual* truth. Interest in the Hills' case **waned** throughout the 1960s, but the Hills were not forgotten entirely; the abduction craze eventually resurfaced in full force. Aliens, whether real or fictional, short-
55   and-gray, or enormous-and-slimy, are imbedded in our culture, so watch the skies!

1. The Hills were a married couple who
    A. encountered strange creatures in the sky.
    B. claimed to have evidence of aliens.
    C. did not believe their own experiences.
    D. claimed to have been abducted by beings from a UFO.
    E. wrecked their car in the White Mountains.

2.   As used in line 29, *viable* most nearly means
    A. central.
    B. physical.
    C. feasible.
    D. irrefutable.
    E. overwhelming.

3.   According to the passage, Betty's star map is
    A. the first thing the Hills submitted to the National Investigations Committee on Aerial Phenomena (NICAP).
    B. a successful stunt to gain publicity, money, and movie rights.
    C. a perfect representation of the Andromeda system.
    D. an encrypted message warning the government of an impending invasion.
    E. a portrayal of a star system that Betty could not have known about.

4. As used in line 52, *waned* most nearly means
    A. vanished.
    B. faded.
    C. grew.
    D. stagnated.
    E. changed.

5. Which choice *best* paraphrases the psychiatrist's main point?
    A. Aliens have no place in science.
    B. Hypnosis is not an entirely dependable method of acquiring the truth.
    C. Hypnosis is reliable for getting facts, but not what people believe to be facts.
    D. People always tell the truth when under hypnosis.
    E. Hypnosis can be used for both good and evil purposes.

Lesson Six

1. **adjacent** (ə jā´ sənt) *adj.* lying near; adjoining
   For lunch, Tim usually walks to the pizza shop *adjacent* to his office building.
   syn: bordering; neighboring   *ant: distant; separate*

2. **candor** (kan´ dər) *n.* sincerity; honesty
   The executive wanted an assistant with enough *candor* to admit that the company had obvious weaknesses.
   syn: frankness; truthfulness   *ant: betrayal; deception*

3. **compassion** (kəm pa´ shun) *n.* awareness and sympathy for the suffering of another
   Bob felt *compassion* for the homeless child, because he, too, once lived on the streets.
   syn: pity; sympathy   *ant: disdain; scorn*

4. **democratic** (dem ə krat´ ik) *adj.* of or for the people; pertaining to government by the people
   The class had a *democratic* election in which the majority of votes determined the homecoming queen.
   syn: egalitarian   *ant: dictatorial; autocratic*

5. **disperse** (di spûrs´) *v.* to scatter; to distribute
   The crowd *dispersed* when the police arrived at the crime scene.
   syn: disband; diffuse; spread   *ant: congregate; gather*

6. **doleful** (dōl´ fəl) *adj.* causing grief; sad
   Brian wore a *doleful* expression on the day of the funeral.
   syn: miserable; wretched   *ant: cheerful; joyful*

7. **duress** (dōō res´) *n.* a threat of harm forcing someone to act against his or her will
   The judge declared the confession inadmissible because it was obtained while the suspect was under *duress*.
   syn: coercion; pressure   *ant: freedom; liberty*

8. **irk** (ûrk) *v.* to annoy; to irritate
   The customer's loud cell phone conversation *irked* everyone in the restaurant.
   syn: vex; bother   *ant: delight; soothe*

9. **ratify** (rat´ ə fī) *v.* to approve formally; to sanction
The town council decided to *ratify* the new bill during the monthly meeting.
syn: authorize; endorse   *ant: veto; prohibit*

10. **sobriety** (sə brī´ i tē) *n.* 1. a seriousness in manner
                     2. a state of abstinence from drugs or alcohol
(1) The *sobriety* of the main character in the movie bored most audiences.
(2) Workers at the factory must maintain total *sobriety* while on duty.
(1) *syn: solemnity; gravity*   *ant: foolishness; impertinence*
(2) *syn: temperance*   *ant: intoxication*

11. **stagnate** (stag´ nāt) *v.* to become inactive or motionless
Business will *stagnate* for companies that do not advertise.
syn: idle; cease   *ant: flourish; grow*

12. **subordinate** (sə bôr´ dn it) *adj.* of lower importance or rank; subject
                     to the control of another
                 n. one who is under the control of another
(adj) The *subordinate* officer receives her orders from the commander.
(n) As manager, Hector has five *subordinates* to train and supervise.
(adj) *syn: dependent; lesser*   *ant: foremost; chief*
(n) *syn: assistant; underling*   *ant: boss; leader*

13. **talon** (tal´ ən) *n.* a claw of a bird of prey or similar animal
The rabbit could not escape the eagle's *talons*.

14. **taut** (tôt) *adj.* pulled, drawn, or stretched tight
Taut ropes ensured the circus tent did not blow away.
syn: rigid; firm   *ant: loose; slack*

15. **wallow** (wol´ ō) *v.* to roll about in something unclean
After the pigs eat, they *wallow* in the muddy pen.

EXERCISE I – Words in Context

Using the vocabulary list for this lesson, supply the correct word to complete each sentence.

1. In a[n] _____ election, the majority of voters decide the outcome.

2. Hank used a spreader to _____ grass seeds all over the front lawn.

3. The new budget proposal will go into effect when the committee _____ it.

4. Dave gave a blunt answer to her question, and she appreciated his _____.

5. A mind will _____ if it is not challenged regularly.

6. Caleb's squeaky chair _____ his classmates.

7. When his fishing line became _____, Allen knew that a fish had taken the bait.

8. The owl used its _____ to capture a mouse.

9. The manager is responsible for three _____.

10. No one bought the nice house because it is _____ to a mosquito-infested swamp.

11. His joke failed to ease the overwhelming atmosphere of _____ in the hospital waiting room.

12. The homeless teenager relied on the _____ of strangers for food and shelter.

13. To keep cool, the hippopotamus _____ in the mud.

14. While the armed robber hid behind the store counter, the clerk winked at the police officer to signal that she was under _____.

15. The _____ song brought a tear to her eye.

EXERCISE II – Sentence Completion

Complete the sentence in a way that shows you understand the meaning of the italicized vocabulary word.

1. She has the *compassion* necessary to...

2. She knew that opening a sandwich shop *adjacent* to the large office building was...

3. If the dripping faucet *irks* someone enough, then he or she might...

4. She smiled, but her *doleful* eyes revealed...

5. In a display of impressive *candor*, Sean admitted...

6. If the lines holding the sails are not pulled *taut*, the wind will...

7. The water in the stream will *stagnate* if...

8. If the family dog *wallows* in the pond, it will...

9. The boss asked her *subordinate* to...

10. Several council members refused to *ratify* the bill unless...

11. The falcon used its sharp *talons* to...

12. The feeding crows *dispersed* when...

13. To reduce the usual *sobriety* of the business meeting, the boss...

14. The bank clerk was under *duress* while the robbers...

15. Someone can tamper with a *democratic* election by...

EXERCISE III – Prefixes and Suffixes

Study the entries and use them to complete the questions that follow.

The suffix *-able* means "able to be."
The suffix *-ate* means "to become" or "to cause to become."
The suffix *-ation* means "act of" or "result of."
The suffix *-some* means "tending to."

Use the provided prefixes and suffixes to change each word so that it completes the sentence correctly. Then, keeping in mind that prefixes and suffixes sometimes change the part of speech, identify the part of speech of the new word by circling N for a noun, V for a verb, or ADJ for an adjective.

1. (duress) The exhausted child slept for the _____ of the trip.

    N   V   ADJ

2. (irk) The picnic was nice except for the _____ flies.

    N   V   ADJ

3. (compassion) Though it is not in the company policy, the _____ manager gives workers extra days off if their family members die.

    N   V   ADJ

4. (duress) The architect designed _____ buildings that could withstand earthquakes.

    N   V   ADJ

EXERCISE IV – Improving Paragraphs

Read the following passage and then answer the multiple-choice questions that follow. The questions will require you to make decisions regarding the revision of the reading selection.

(1) In the year AD 386, Chinese astronomers saw a tiny flash in the night sky. (2) The point of light grew in intensity until it was visible even during the day. (3) The astronomers called the light a "guest star." (4) Within a year, the light from the "visitor," as the Chinese also referred to it, could no longer be seen. (5) The light was no longer visible to the naked eye. (6) But what had the ancients just witnessed?

(7) Modern scientists presume that the ancients saw a supernova, the explosion that occurs when certain stars die. (8) The event begins when the fusion of a star **stagnates** after billions of years of consuming the star's fuel. (9) Lighter elements in the star, such as hydrogen and helium, fuse together to form heavier elements such as carbon and oxygen. (10) Fusion continues until the point in which most of the elements have been converted to iron and cannot be burned by the star, which stops burning.

(11) When fusion stops, the star collapses in on itself, forcing the core into a super-dense orb only a few miles in diameter (remember, it contains all the matter of the star—upwards of one million planet Earths). (12) In seconds, under unimaginable pressure, the core heats to billions of degrees and the outer portion explodes, releasing more energy than a billion nuclear bombs. (13) The explosion is so great that it affects **subordinate** stars in the region, sometimes completely destroying the smaller ones, and the blast produces the light of a billion stars put together.

(14) Interestingly, the very center of the star, or core, remains intact after the explosion. (15) The compact star is so dense that objects would need to travel at near light-speed to escape its gravity. (16) Also, neutron stars sometimes spin very rapidly, up to thirty or forty times per second (remember that Earth rotates just once in twenty four hours)! (17) These spinning neutron stars are called *pulsars*.

(18) The spinning pulsar has a powerful magnetic field that generates X-rays, so even though the light from the supernova **dispersed** throughout the centuries, scientists can still detect the remnants of the AD 386 supernova using X-ray telescopes.

(19) The discovery of the pulsar was especially significant because it prompted scientists to reconsider the way in which they estimate the age of neutron stars. (20) Before the pulsar was found to be in the nebula created by the 386 AD supernova, it was estimated to be 24,000 years old.(21) Now, thanks the Chinese astronomers' original observation, scientists estimate the pulsar to be a youthful 1,600 years. (22) The ancients likely would have been thrilled to know their records are useful nearly two millennia later, but they probably would be more thrilled to learn that the point of light they saw was actually a distant event of a scale beyond even the modern scientist's imagination.

1. Which sentence should be deleted because it is redundant?
    A. sentence 3
    B. sentence 5
    C. sentence 7
    D. sentence 9
    E. sentence 11

2. Of the following choices, which is the best revision of sentence 10 (printed below)?

    > Fusion continues until the point in which
    > most of the elements have been converted to
    > iron and cannot be burned by the star, which
    > stops burning.

    A. Fusion continues until the point is reached in which most of the elements have been converted to iron and the star can no longer burn.
    B. The fusion stops when the star is all iron and cannot burn.
    C. The fusion stops when the point has been reached in which the elements are all fused into iron and the star cannot keep burning them.
    D. The elements soon stop fusion because the iron can no longer be burned by the star and it stops burning.
    E. The fusion continues until most of the elements have been converted to iron, and the star can no longer burn.

3. Which sentence should be added to follow sentence 14?
    A. A neutron star has been formed.
    B. The remnant is left over after the massive explosion.
    C. Do not confuse the remnant as being a *neutron star*.
    D. We call this remnant a *compact*, or *neutron*, star.
    E. Why does this happen?

4. This writer of this passage does not attempt to
    A. link ancient astronomy to modern science.
    B. explain the cause of a celestial event.
    C. introduce new theories of star formation.
    D. pose questions to the reader.
    E. illustrate a development in star dating.

Review

Lessons 4 – 6

EXERCISE I – Inferences

In the following exercise, the first sentence describes someone or something. Infer information from the first sentence, and then choose the word from the Word Bank that best completes the second sentence.

Word Bank

doleful	superficial	nominal	terrestrial
adjacent	obstinate	vapid	subordinate

1. The nation has a king, but the prime minister makes all the important decisions.
   From this sentence, we can infer that king is a[n] _____ position.

2. Though the fire started in the sporting-goods store, the blaze quickly spread to the neighboring frozen-yogurt shop.
   From this sentence, we can infer that the frozen-yogurt shop was _____ to the sporting-goods store.

3. Every six months, Jim and his coworkers receive performance evaluations from Mr. Porter.
   From this sentence, we can infer that Jim is a[n] _____ of Mr. Porter.

4. When her mother tried to feed her, the little girl squirmed in her high chair, shook her head, and kept her mouth clamped shut.
   From this sentence, we can infer that the child is _____.

5. Wanda said that she will marry anyone as long as he is handsome and rich.
   From this sentence, we can infer that Wanda is _____.

EXERCISE II – Related Words

Some of the vocabulary words from lessons 4–6 have related meanings. Complete the following sentences by choosing the word that best completes the specified relationship. Some word pairs will be antonyms, some will be synonyms, and some will be words often used in the same context.

1. *Nurture* is opposite in meaning to the word
    A. compassion.
    B. eavesdrop.
    C. candor.
    D. stunt.
    E. ratify.

2. *Irrelevant* is nearest in meaning to
    A. seismic.
    B. dynamic.
    C. viable.
    D. ethical.
    E. superficial.

3. Something that is *ultimate* is not likely to be
    A. nominal.
    B. taut.
    C. adjacent.
    D. viable.
    E. durable.

4. A *viable* plan must be _____ enough to withstand changes and criticism.
    A. bizarre
    B. stagnate
    C. durable
    D. vapid
    E. terrestrial

5. *Gaudy* contrasts most with the word
    A. nominal.
    B. vapid.
    C. obstinate.
    D. adjacent.
    E. superficial.

6. If someone has a *wan* expression, then he or she likely could be
   A. superficial.
   B. durable.
   C. doleful.
   D. dynamic.
   E. viable.

7. Relief from *duress* could occur during periods of
   A. candor.
   B. quibbles.
   C. rites.
   D. stunts.
   E. respite.

8. If interest in the show *wanes*, then the people in the crowd are likely to
   A. wallow.
   B. ratify.
   C. disperse.
   D. pommel.
   E. bungle.

9. If a singer continuously fails to provide *dynamic* performances, then his or her career will
   A. stagnate.
   B. eavesdrop.
   C. disperse.
   D. loiter.
   E. irk.

10. A *seismic* disturbance is often _____ in origin.
    A. taut
    B. fjord
    C. adjacent
    D. terrestrial
    E. acute

EXERCISE III – Crossword Puzzle

Use the clues to complete the crossword puzzle. The answers consist of vocabulary words from lessons 4 through 6.

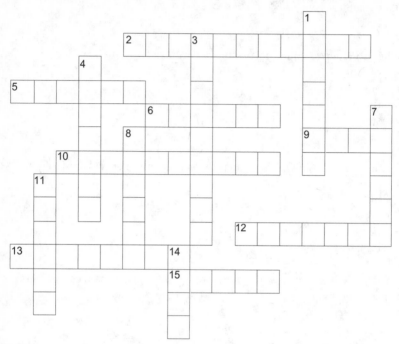

Across

2. The manager promised her _____[s] that she would take full responsibility for the accident.
5. Police asked curious bystanders not to _____ around the scene of the accident.
6. The committee will _____ the new charter if no one has any objections.
9. Guests bowed their heads in silent reflection during the funeral _____.
10. The doctor will _____ the patient's record before prescribing any medication.
12. Please resolve your differences now, because we will not have time to _____ during the game.
13. The classroom was chilly, so Tina sat at the desk _____ to the heater.
15. Charlie blamed the seafood dinner for his _____ case of food poisoning.

Down

1. Soldiers were forced to abandon the _____[s] when their food supply ran out.
3. The _____ salesman refused to reduce the price of the used car.
4. The doctor knows that it is not _____ to give out the names of his patients.
7. The fire marshal was able to _____ the cause of the fire by looking at the electrical box.
8. Tanya _____[ed] the delivery by accidentally leaving the package at the bus station.
11. With great _____, the owner of the company explained to the employees that the business would be bankrupt in less than a year.
14. If the support line is not _____, the tent will flap in the wind.

Lesson Seven

1. **badger** (baj´ ər) *v.* to harass persistently; to annoy
    The bear cubs *badgered* their mother for milk.
    syn: pester; hassle   *ant: delight; please*

2. **benevolent** (bə nev´ ə lənt) *adj.* showing, doing, or resulting in good;
    kindhearted
    The *benevolent* organization sold baked goods to raise money for charity.
    syn: compassionate; generous   *ant: selfish; mean*

3. **elapse** (i laps´) *v.* to slip by, as in time
    Barely one hour had *elapsed* before police caught the burglar.
    syn: pass

4. **fitful** (fit´ fəl) *adj.* stopping and starting intermittently
    Paul fell into a *fitful* sleep after being bitten by the snake.
    syn: erratic; irregular   *ant: constant; steady*

5. **genre** (zhän´ rə) *n.* a category; a type
    Of the many *genres* of literature, I enjoy science fiction the most.
    syn: sort; class

6. **haven** (hā´ vən) *n.* a place of safety; a sanctuary
    The abandoned warehouse eventually became a winter *haven* for the
    homeless.
    syn: refuge; shelter

7. **immaterial** (im mə tir´ ē əl) *adj.* of little or no importance; irrelevant
    The judge dismissed the evidence because it was *immaterial* to the case.
    syn: unimportant; insignificant   *ant: pertinent; applicable*

8. **innate** (in´ āt) *adj.* possessed from birth; inborn; inherent
    Science has not yet determined whether mathematical ability is *innate* or
    learned.
    syn: instinctive; hereditary   *ant: acquired; learned*

9. **kindle** (kin´ dl) *v.* 1. to set fire to; to catch fire
                             2. to arouse feelings; to stir emotion
    (1) The hiker *kindled* a good cooking fire using only a single match.
    (2) The massive dinosaur skeletons at the museum *kindled* the student's
         curiosity.
    (1) *syn: ignite*   *ant: extinguish*
    (2) *syn: stimulate; provoke*   *ant: quench; suppress*

10. **listless** (list´ lis) *adj.* lacking energy; unenthusiastic
The injured, *listless* puppy cried pitifully.
syn: lethargic   *ant: energetic; animated*

11. **meager** (mē´ gər) *adj.* lacking abundance; inadequate; scanty
The *meager* rations barely kept the prisoners alive.
syn: paltry; insufficient   *ant: ample; sufficient*

12. **octogenarian** (ok tə jə när´ ē ən) *n.* someone between eighty and eighty-nine years old
Some *octogenarians* are in better health than middle-aged people.

13. **permeate** (pûr´ mē āt) *v.* to spread or flow through; to penetrate throughout
Gasoline fumes *permeated* the rags, making them extremely flammable.

14. **republic** (ri pub´ lik) *n.* a government in which citizens elect officials to represent them
The United States is a constitutional *republic*, not a democracy.

15. **tether** (teth´ ər) *n.* a rope or chain used to restrain
                                      v. to use a rope or chain to restrain
(n) The pilot of the hot air balloon cut the *tether* and began her flight.
(v) The watchman *tethered* the guard dog to the main entrance gate.
(v) *syn: fasten; secure*   *ant: release; liberate*

EXERCISE I – Words in Context

Using the vocabulary list for this lesson, supply the correct word to complete each sentence.

1. The thin jacket provided _____ protection against the sub-zero temperatures.

2. The teacher included mystery, science fiction, and historical fiction in the class's study of literary _____.

3. His assertion was right, but it did not help his team at all because his point was _____ to the subject of the debate.

4. Please take the burning pot roast outside before the smoke _____ everything in the house.

5. The fugitive found a temporary _____ at the home of a distant relative.

6. The old photographs evoked memories of her childhood and _____ feelings of love and acceptance.

7. Scott _____ the celebrity for an autograph until her bodyguards threw him out.

8. In its time, the Roman _____ was the most powerful nation in the world.

9. He had a[n] _____ expression, but a dark secret lurked deep within.

10. Vince, a mountain climber, claims to have a[n] _____ need to be in high places.

11. The cowboy _____ his horse to the hitching post in front of the saloon.

12. After the long class, the students reacted with _____ groans when the teacher assigned additional homework.

13. Please wait for twenty minutes to _____ before you check the roast in the oven.

14. Their _____ whispering during the movie annoyed everyone in the theater.

15. The _____ experienced two world wars and hundreds of technological advancements during his long and fascinating life.

EXERCISE II – Sentence Completion

Complete the sentence in a way that shows you understand the meaning of the italicized vocabulary word.

1. If you like the fiction *genre*, then you will enjoy…

2. Sandra is *listless* in the morning until she…

3. He demonstrated his *benevolent* intentions by…

4. If you include too many *immaterial* facts during your oral report, you might…

5. *Octogenarians* can tell you stories about…

6. One good way to *kindle* interest in a subject is…

7. Mosquitoes *badgered* the campers until…

8. Please allow at least twenty minutes to *elapse* before you…

9. Some animals have the *innate* ability to…

10. Our *meager* supplies will not…

11. At night, the stray cat found a *haven* in…

12. If you put a sliced onion in the refrigerator, the odor will *permeate*…

13. Billy *tethered* his bike to the fence so…

14. Citizens of the *republic* are expected to…

15. They experienced a brief period of *fitful* coughing after…

EXERCISE III – Prefixes and Suffixes

Study the entries and use them to complete the questions that follow.

The prefix *sub-* means "under" or "beneath."
The suffix *-able* means "able to be."
The suffix *-ize* means "to become" or "to cause to become."
The suffix *-ness* means "state," "quality," or "condition."

Use the provided prefixes and suffixes to change each word so that it completes the sentence correctly. Then, keeping in mind that prefixes and suffixes sometimes change the part of speech, identify the part of speech of the new word by circling N for a noun, V for a verb, or ADJ for an adjective.

1. (immaterial) The detective will _____ any clues that do not assist the investigation.

    N   V   ADJ

2. (permeate) A jacket made of _____ material will not keep the wearer dry in the rain.

    N   V   ADJ

3. (meager) The _____ of the water supply during the drought prompted the city government to enforce restrictions on water usage.

    N   V   ADJ

4. (genre) The horror novel is a popular _____ of fiction.

    N   V   ADJ

EXERCISE IV – Critical Reading

The following reading passage contains vocabulary words from this lesson. Carefully read the passage and then choose the best answers for each of the questions that follow.

1   Scientists can tell us when, to the minute, comets will pass through our solar system, and physicists can describe the behavior of subatomic particles so tiny that they barely seem to exist, but no one can explain why a simple insect, the monarch butterfly, is able to navigate to a destination one thousand miles away when it has never before made the journey.

2   In late August, somewhere in the northern United States, a beautiful orange-and-black female lays a single egg upon a milkweed plant. She then flies to a new plant and does it again; she repeats the sequence more than one hundred times. After two months **elapse**, the eggs hatch, the larvae grow into adult butterflies, and then, remarkably, they join millions of other monarchs in making a journey to Mexico—a **haven** during the winter.

3   During the trip, the butterflies endure high winds, extreme heat and cold, hungry predators, and **meager** nourishment received through the nectar of flowers; however, their **innate** drive to find a suitable place to wait out the winter forces them to continue. A slew of monarchs eventually arrives in Mexico, and the exhausted insects rest in trees, their number so great that branches sometimes snap under the burden.

4   How the butterflies make the arduous journey with neither compass nor map is still a mystery. The moon and stars cannot be factors because monarchs become **listless** in the dark and do not fly. Neither do butterflies have internal compasses like migratory birds; tests have proven that monarchs are not sensitive to the earth's magnetic field. The journey is not a learned behavior, because parent butterflies teach nothing to the offspring. The ability certainly has nothing to do with human influence because the butterflies have been soaring along the same routes for millions of years.

5   One possible explanation is that monarchs follow natural landmarks, such as mountains and rivers, but how the monarchs would understand the significance of the landmarks is anyone's guess. The many theories of monarch navigation **kindle** fierce debates within the scientific community, but even in the twenty-first century, no one can make a definite conclusion.

6   To people who love butterflies simply for their beauty, the secret of monarch navigation is **immaterial**. Few insects are as eye-catching as a black-and-orange monarch resting on a porch rail, dazzling watchers with its delicacy and contrast. Knowing that the quiet creature is capable of international travel is hardly necessary for someone to appreciate it.

1. Which choice most accurately paraphrases the first paragraph?
    A. Only astrologers and physicists can truly understand butterflies.
    B. Butterflies have a strange atomic structure.
    C. The simplest things are sometimes the most difficult to understand.
    D. Comets probably affect the migration patterns of butterflies.
    E. Butterflies have perplexed humans for thousands of years.

2. As used in paragraph 3, *meager* most nearly means
    A. scanty.
    B. insufficient.
    C. wasteful.
    D. ample.
    E. listless.

3. The passage offers which choice as a possible explanation of the butterfly's ability to navigate?
    A. Butterflies teach their offspring how to make the journey.
    B. Butterflies follow the natural geography of the earth.
    C. Humanity forces the butterfly to use specific routes.
    D. Butterflies seek sources of milkweed for reproduction.
    E. Butterflies navigate by the moon and stars.

4. As used in paragraph 5, *kindle* most nearly means the opposite of
    A. extinguish.
    B. ignite.
    C. provoke.
    D. end.
    E. settle.

5. The author of this passage would probably agree with which statement?
    A. Without science, the world has little happiness.
    B. One need not understand nature to enjoy it.
    C. Butterflies are nothing compared to comets and nuclear physics.
    D. The secret of how butterflies reproduce might never be known.
    E. Butterflies will change their migratory habits eventually.

Lesson Eight

1. **alight** (ə līt´) v. to descend and settle, as after flying
             adj. burning; lighted
    (v) Jennifer watched a cardinal *alight* upon the bench outside her window.
    (adj) Awakened by the smell of smoke, he looked outside and saw the barn *alight*.
    (v) *syn: land; perch; come down*   *ant: fly; rocket; take off*
    (adj) *syn: ablaze; flaming*   *ant: extinguished*

2. **convalesce** (kon´ və les) v. to recover one's health
    Tom had a long period to *convalesce* after the car accident.
    syn: recuperate; rehabilitate   *ant: weaken; deteriorate*

3. **dainty** (dān´ tē) adj. preciously delicate or charming
    Eileen stores her *dainty*, crystal figurines in a glass display case, away from her children's curious hands.
    syn: fragile; elegant; pretty   *ant: ungainly; burly*

4. **feint** (fānt) v. to distract an opponent by pretending to move in one direction and then moving in another
             n. a deceptive act meant to distract or deceive one's opponent
    (v) The boxer *feinted* to the right to throw his opponent off guard, and then struck him with a sharp left hook.
    (n) The swordsman did not fall for the villain's *feint*.
    (v) *syn: fake; bluff*
    (n) *syn: cheat; facade*

5. **implore** (im plôr´) v. to beg
    Theresa *implored* the king to spare her brother, who was caught spying.
    syn: entreat; plead   *ant: order; command*

6. **impugn** (im pyōōn´) v. to attack as false; to cast doubt on
    The prosecutor *impugned* the defendant's alibi at every available opportunity.
    syn: contradict; oppose   *ant: support; defend*

7. **integral** (in´ ti grəl) adj. necessary to make something complete; essential
    Daily practice is *integral* to a successful season.
    syn: central; key   *ant: optional*

8. **jurisdiction** (jŏŏr is dik´ shən)   *n.*   1. the authority to interpret and apply the law   2. the geographical range of an authority
    (1) The state trooper does not have the *jurisdiction* to arrest people in the neighboring state.
    (2) The suspect escaped punishment by fleeing the detective's *jurisdiction*.
    (1) *syn: power; rule; influence*
    (2) *syn: scope; reach*

9. **malnutrition** (mal nōō trish´ ən)   *n.*   a lack of proper nutrition
    The castaway knew that he would suffer from *malnutrition* if he did not find something other than coconuts to eat.
    syn: undernourishment; famine

10. **meddle** (med´ dəl)   *v.*   to intrude in the business of others; to interfere
    Mrs. Thompson told her children not to *meddle* in the affairs of strangers.
    syn: pry; snoop   *ant: ignore; overlook*

11. **painstaking** (pānz´ tāk ing)   *adj.*   using or requiring great care and effort
    After ten years of *painstaking* research, the scientist finally made a break-through.
    syn: meticulous; diligent   *ant: careless; negligent*

12. **pantheon** (pan´ thē on)   *n.*   1. a group of highly regarded people
                                        2. a place dedicated to highly regarded people
    (1) The Nobel Prize *pantheon* includes such people as Marie Curie and Albert Einstein.
    (2) The art museum is a *pantheon* of the greatest artists in history.

13. **sear** (sēr)   *v.*   1. to scorch or burn the surface of
                            2. to make dry and withered
    (v.1) To *sear* the meat, the chef turned the flame up on the grill.
    (v.2) During the heat wave, the sun *seared* the leaves of the delicate tree.
    (v.1) *syn: singe; char*
    (v.2) *syn: parch; dehydrate*   *ant: moisten; dampen*

14. **vertical** (vûr´ tik əl)   *adj.*   perpendicular to the horizon
    A *vertical* column of water shot into the air after Tim's car struck the fire hydrant.
    syn: upright; erect   *ant: horizontal; flat*

15. **wince** (wins)   *v.*   to flinch
    Dominic *winced* when he saw the antique vase fall from the shelf.
    syn: cringe; recoil

EXERCISE I – Words in Context

Using the vocabulary list for this lesson, supply the correct word to complete each sentence.

1. Lucas _____ the landlord to give him another week to pay the rent.

2. A steady diet of potato chips and cola will soon result in _____ and obesity.

3. Dr. Insano hates it when Captain Freedom _____ with his mad plans to take over the world.

4. The bird will not _____ until it sees food on the ground.

5. The artist at the knickknack factory has the _____ job of painting tiny details on each of the figurines.

6. Julia's friends visited her at the hospital while she _____ from the illness.

7. On top of the music box is a[n] _____ ballerina that rotates as the song plays.

8. The first step is _____ to the whole process, so please remember to do it.

9. The bridge sits atop ten _____ pilings that extend deep into the water.

10. The hot sun will _____ the grapes until they turn into raisins.

11. Ralph _____ to the left, evading the players trying to tackle him.

12. The Baseball Hall of Fame is a[n] _____ dedicated to the greatest players in history.

13. Officer Brad did not give Heather a speeding ticket this time, but he warned her not to get caught speeding in his _____ again.

14. Carly _____ when she saw the silly expression on her face in her embarrassing yearbook photograph.

15. The court _____ Charlotte after agents caught her selling secret documents to an enemy spy.

EXERCISE II – Sentence Completion

Complete the sentence in a way that shows you understand the meaning of the italicized vocabulary word.

1. The *pantheon* contained statues of...

2. If the boss *meddles* with the vacation schedule, the workers might...

3. You will need several weeks to *convalesce* if...

4. The pigeons will *alight* on the lawn if you...

5. She knew the *feint* had worked when she...

6. When the thief escaped her *jurisdiction*, the sheriff had to...

7. Fred *winced* when...

8. Rachel *impugned* her son's story that he simply misplaced his new toy because...

9. Exercise and proper nutrition are *integral* to...

10. Phillip *implored* his parents to...

11. No one thought the *dainty* woman would...

12. One way to avoid *malnutrition* is...

13. The reporter saw rows of *vertical* bars as he walked through...

14. The flame of the blowtorch *seared*...

15. Hunter did not want the *painstaking* job of...

EXERCISE III – Prefixes and Suffixes

Study the entries and use them to complete the questions that follow.

The suffix -*ate* means "to become" or "to cause to become."
The suffix -*ence* means "state of" or "quality of."
The suffix -*ent* means "performer of."
The suffix -*ity* means "state of" or "quality of."

Use the provided prefixes and suffixes to change each word so that it completes the sentence correctly. Then, keeping in mind that prefixes and suffixes sometimes change the part of speech, identify the part of speech of the new word by circling N for a noun, V for a verb, or ADJ for an adjective.

1. (convalesce) The doctor ordered Chloe to stay in bed during her
    _____.   N   V   ADJ

2. (integral) Someone who always does what he or she knows to be right is
    said to have _____.   N   V   ADJ

3. (convalesce) Owing a shortage of hospital beds, some _____ were
    asked to finish recovering at home.   N   V   ADJ

4. (integral) Several automakers now _____ global positioning systems
    into their automobiles.   N   V   ADJ

EXERCISE IV – Critical Reading

The following reading passage contains vocabulary words from this lesson. Carefully read the passage and then choose the best answers for each of the questions that follow.

On December 26ᵗʰ, 2004, just before 8:00 am, an earthquake measuring 9.0 on the Richter scale rumbled the Nicobar Islands in the Indian Ocean near the northern coast of Sumatra. A quake of this magnitude occurs about once every twenty years; the last to come close was a 9.2 that struck Prince
5   William Sound in 1964. Like most earthquakes, the Indian Ocean earthquake was caused by shifting tectonic plates—the vast, broken "pieces" that form the outer portion of Earth's crust; however, this earthquake was just the beginning of a more far-reaching disaster.

When the two plates collided near Nicobar, one plate wedged slightly
10   beneath the other. It seems insignificant until you consider the enormousness of the plates—they are foundations of continents, miles deep and made of rock. When the edges of the plates met, the collision released huge amounts of energy, causing the seafloor and water above the fault to rise. The energy thrust billions of tons of seawater upward, causing a **vertical** "bulge" of water
15   on the surface.

The bulge, enormous but barely perceptible to people on the surface, immediately plunged back into the ocean, causing waves to travel outward at speeds upward of 400 miles per hour. Despite their great energy, the waves were of little height, so ships far from shore barely noticed them passing. It
20   was different, however, for people on the coast.

They noticed a drop in the tide. Not realizing that the water had moved out to sea to fill the gap created by the approaching wave of destruction, adults and children ran onto the beach to collect fish left flopping on the seabed.

25   As the waves approached the shore, the resistance of the shallow water caused them to compress. They lost speed, but built upon one another and increased in amplitude until they reached heights approaching 100 feet. The wave's length increased the impending devastation. The wave, from one crest to the next, was miles long. This was not some **dainty** tidal wave that crashed
30   onto the beach and swept some umbrellas away—this was several *minutes* of one *single, enormous, continuous* wave that had no intention of stopping when it hit the coast.

The epic surge snapped trees in half, leveled buildings, and swept tens of thousands of people beneath the foam as it pushed inland as far as a mile.
35   When the water receded, debris littered thousands of miles of coastline. Automobiles lay overturned, streets had turned into rivers, and victims desperately sought missing friends and family members. The death toll, initially estimated at 100,000, climbed during the **painstaking** recovery, passing 160,000. It was the deadliest tsunami in recorded history.

40   Everyone had been caught off guard. Unlike natives of Japan, where tidal waves are common and sudden changes in the tide are carefully watched, few people on the coast of the Indian Ocean knew the warning signs. Seismologists detected the earthquake hours before the wave, but no one knew whom to contact. Because of the rarity of tsunamis in the Indian Ocean, most of the

45   stricken areas were outside the warning center's **jurisdiction**. Agencies now agree that an effective warning system will be **integral** to protecting the coast from future tsunamis.

1.   According to the passage, which of the following is a sign of an approaching tsunami?
    A. an earthquake
    B. a sudden drop in water level
    C. low speed but constant breeze
    D. tectonic plate activity
    E. fish jumping from the water

2.   According to the passage, a tsunami wave near its starting point could
    A. wipe out an entire fleet of battleships.
    B. collide with other waves and simply cancel itself out.
    C. be as tall as 100 feet.
    D. pass by a ship undetected.
    E. replenish coral reefs in the area.

3.   As used in line 29, *dainty* most nearly means
    A. devastating.
    B. strong.
    C. fragile.
    D. delicate.
    E. slight.

4.   Which choice would be the most appropriate title for the passage?
    A. The Largest Earthquake in History
    B. A Two-Part Disaster: the Indian Ocean Earthquake, Tsunami, and Recovery
    C. Surviving Earthquakes and Tsunamis
    D. Disaster from the Deep
    E. Earthquakes and Tsunamis

5.   As used in line 46, *integral* most nearly means
      A.   detrimental.
      B.   supportive.
      C.   essential.
      D.   secondary.
      E.   ideal.

Lesson Nine

1. **antagonist** (an tag´ ō nist) *n.* someone who opposes another; an adversary
The *antagonist* of the play constantly interferes with the hero's intentions.
syn: enemy; opponent   *ant: supporter; advocate; friend*

2. **detriment** (det´ rə mənt) *n.* a disadvantage; a loss
The injury was a *detriment* to the player's future in sports.
syn: drawback; handicap; impairment   *ant: advantage; benefit; asset*

3. **drone** (drōn) *v.* to speak in a montonous tone
            n. 1. a person who does menial, tedious work
                 2. a continuous, dull sound
(v) The boring lecturer *droned* on about the subject for what felt like hours.
(n.1) After years of repetitive work, he felt like a *drone* whose employee number was more significant than his name.
(n.2) The house was silent except for the *drone* of the air conditioner.
(n.1) *syn: lackey; minion*   *ant: boss; leader*

4. **drudgery** (druj´ ə rē) *n.* tedious, wearisome work
Dan wanted to plant trees in the front yard, but he did not want the *drudgery* of digging holes for the next five days.
syn: labor; toil

5. **horizontal** (hôr ə zon´ təl) *adj.* parallel to the horizon; level
Ted wore a polo shirt decorated with *horizontal* stripes.
syn: flat; straight   *ant: vertical; upright*

6. **hypocrite** (hip´ ə krit) *n.* a person who does not practice the beliefs or opinions that he or she professes
The celebrity was a *hypocrite* who bought pleasure yachts and summer mansions while writing songs about the importance of giving away worldly possessions.

7. **insubordinate** (in sə bôr´ dn it) *adj.* defiant to authority; disobedient; rebellious
The sergeant ordered the *insubordinate* soldier to buff the floors of the barracks.
syn: resistant; unruly   *ant: obedient; respectful*

8. **mentor** (men´ tôr) *n.* a wise, trusted counselor or advisor
Jamie aimed to model her career after that of her *mentor*.
syn: teacher; confidant

9. **oration** (ôr ā´ shən) *n.* an elaborate, formal speech
Members of the audience were captivated by the speaker's well-delivered *oration*.
syn: lecture; sermon

10. **retract** (ri trakt´) *v.* 1. to draw back or in
                                2. to disavow a belief or statement
(1) Be sure you *retract* the tip of that pen before you set it on the couch.
(2) He *retracted* his statement after he received numerous threats to his life.
(1) *syn: withdraw*   *ant: project*
(2) *syn: revoke; repeal*   *ant: uphold; sustain*

11. **sanctuary** (sāngk´ chōō er ē) *n.* 1. a place of refuge or safety
                                          2. a sacred place
(1) A dozen species of birds nest in the wildlife *sanctuary*.
(2) Religious services are conducted in the *sanctuary*.
(1) *syn: asylum; shelter; haven*

12. **scamper** (skam´ pûr) *v.* to run lightly and hurriedly
The crab *scampered* across the sand, unaware of the seagull above.
syn: scurry; dart   *ant: lumber; trudge*

13. **solace** (sol´ əs) *n.* comfort amid sorrow or trouble
                          v. to comfort; to console
(n) The kind neighbor always provided *solace* when times were difficult.
(v) No one could *solace* her after the flood destroyed everything in her home.
(n) *syn: relief; support*   *ant: irritation; stress*
(v) *syn: soothe*   *ant: depress; dishearten*

14. **somber** (som´ bər) *adj.* dismal; bleak
He painted a *somber* winter landscape showing dead trees and gray skies.
syn: grave; solemn   *ant: cheerful; bright*

15. **zenith** (zē´ nith) *n.* the highest point; the peak
Knowing that she had passed the *zenith* of her career, Nancy decided to retire.
syn: summit; climax   *ant: bottom; nadir*

EXERCISE I – Words in Context

Using the vocabulary list for this lesson, supply the correct word to complete each sentence.

1. The hot weather is a[n] _____ to the people running in the race.

2. At the _____ of her popularity, the star made several public appearances each day.

3. A large spider _____ across the floor and through a crack in the wall.

4. Not one nation offered _____ to the wanted criminal, so he turned himself in.

5. On the morning after the assassination, citizens awoke to the _____ tolling of a funeral bell.

6. The seatbelt should _____ back into the seat after you unbuckle it.

7. If the table surface is not _____, the apples will roll onto the floor.

8. You'll be called a[n] _____ if you do not practice what you preach.

9. The crowd went silent when the guest of honor delivered a moving _____.

10. During the difficult time, Janet was thankful that her friends were present to offer _____.

11. Owing to advancements in technology, few modern Americans can fathom the _____ of working in the early coal mining industry.

12. The _____ prisoner was placed in solitary confinement for fighting with the guards.

13. Lisa learned everything she knew about the job from her _____, who also became her friend.

14. The _____ of the jet engines helped Bob fall asleep during the flight.

15. The _____ of the story tries to thwart the hero's progress.

EXERCISE II – Sentence Completion

Complete the sentence in a way that shows you understand the meaning of the italicized vocabulary word.

1. Janet prefers the *horizontal* landscape of Kansas to…

2. People called him a *hypocrite* because…

3. Even the simplest task will become *drudgery* if…

4. Some fans thought the new player was a *detriment* to the team, while others thought…

5. The teacher told the *insubordinate* student to…

6. Reading the *somber* story caused…

7. Lara's *mentor* advised her about…

8. Jim often retreats to a *sanctuary* in the wilderness where he can…

9. Family members *solaced* Jennifer when…

10. She *retracted* her statement as soon as…

11. During a public *oration*, the mayor explained…

12. From miles away, we heard the *drone* of…

13. Children *scampered* across the field when…

14. The sun is at its *zenith* when…

15. The *antagonist* in the crowd constantly…

EXERCISE III – Prefixes and Suffixes

Study the entries and use them to complete the questions that follow.

The prefix *con-* means "together."
The prefix *ex-* means "out" or "from."
The suffix *-ic* means "characteristic of" or "pertaining to."
The suffix *-ize* means "to become" or "to cause to become."

Use the provided prefixes and suffixes to change each word so that it completes the sentence correctly. Then, keeping in mind that prefixes and suffixes sometimes change the part of speech, identify the part of speech of the new word by circling N for a noun, V for a verb, or ADJ for an adjective.

1. (antagonist) Puppies sometimes _____ the old dog by nipping at its
    ears while it tries to sleep.   N   V   ADJ

2. (retract) The baseball player was found to be in violation of his _____
    with the team when he was caught using steroids.
                                      N   V   ADJ

3. (antagonist) The comedian received more boos than laughs from the
    _____ crowd.   N   V   ADJ

4. (retract) Hummingbirds _____ nectar from flowers with their tube-
    like beaks.   N   V   ADJ

EXERCISE IV – Improving Paragraphs

Read the following passage and then answer the multiple-choice questions that follow. The questions will require you to make decisions regarding the revision of the reading selection.

1   There will always be people who nag you and prod you to "Get with it!" and try the latest fad, be it a diet, a new style of pants, or some miraculous appliance guaranteed to eliminate the **drudgery** of cooking. Hold your ground. No matter how great the new product seems to be, or how many millions of people are using it, do not give in unless you understand what makes the new thing work. If that means putting down your cell phone, passing up the LASIK eye surgery, or using actual sugar in your cookie recipe rather than one of the many available substitutes, then do it, just until you have a little more understanding of the long-term effects. If being the black sheep has you down, you can take **solace** from the story of the radium fad.

2   In 1898, Marie Curie discovered another radioactive element: radium. Scientists of the time knew what radiation was, but they did not yet realize that it could be a great **detriment** to health. With all the talk of energy surrounding radium, most professionals—physicians, scientists, etc.— assumed that radiation, in proper doses, could do only wonderful things to health. The fad was born.

3   In the early twentieth century, radium was believed to cure every malady from high blood pressure to chronic depression. Companies sold the glowing, gamma-ray-emitting element in pill form, liquid, and even infused in patches to be worn on parts of the body.

4   It gets worse. Of all the remedies available, radium water, or "liquid sunshine," was by far the most popular. At the **zenith** of the fad, hundreds of thousands of people were drinking water laced with radium with the belief that it rejuvenated them. Potency of the water varied. Drinking waters contained relatively low levels of radium, while tonics or "medicinal" waters such as Radithor contained hazardous levels. And it was everywhere. Hotels offered radium water to guests, they went to radium spas to soak in radioactive water, and, yes, doctors prescribed it for every disorder imaginable.

5   Few happy patrons realized the dangers of radium until 1927. That is when Grace Fryer filed a lawsuit against her former employer, U.S. Radium. For years, she and many other women used small brushes and radium powder to paint glow-in-the-dark numbers on watches and instruments. The women had been instructed to use their lips to straighten the brushes between strokes. Grace eventually found a new job, but she knew something was wrong when her teeth fell out and she suffered severe bone

decay. Grace and at least five other women died in agony of radiation poisoning. Dozens followed.

6   If Grace Fryer raised suspicions about radium. Eben Byer confirmed them. In 1928, Byer, a steel tycoon, sought treatment for an injury. His doctor prescribed Radithor. For two years, Byer drank several 2-ounce bottles a day. A 1932 Wall Street Journal headline best sums up the result of Byer's treatment: "The Radium Water Worked Fine Until His Jaw Came Off." Byers was 51 years old.

7   The fad ceased, but not before hundreds of other victims of radiation poisoning came forward. Radium-product manufacturers halted production and physicians **retracted** the professed healing powers of the toxic element. Atomic tests of the 1940s soon showed the world the deadly potential of the new radioactive elements, and the **somber** fear of radioactive fallout and contamination has haunted everyone since.

8   Like many lessons, the cost of the radium craze was high, but at least mankind learned another lesson about its vulnerability to the forces of nature, especially the force of a fad.

1.   Which phrase should be added to follow *1898* in paragraph 2? (assume all details in the choices are factual)
       A.   just three years after the discovery of Uranium,
       B.   despite heated controversy over female scientists,
       C.   only twenty years before World War I,
       D.   more than 100 years ago,
       E.   the same year as the Spanish American War,

2.   Which revision best improves the underlined portion of this sentence from paragraph 4?

               Hotels offered radium water to guests, <u>they went to radium spas to soak in radioactive water</u>, and, yes, doctors prescribed it for every disorder imaginable.

       A.   they soaked in radioactive water in spas
       B.   people went to radium spas to soak in radioactive water
       C.   in spas full of radioactive water, people soaked
       D.   in spas, people soaked in radioactive water
       E.   radioactive water was soaked in by them

3. Which choice shows the best way to combine the first two sentences of paragraph 6?
    A. ...radium. Eben Byer...
    B. ...radium, so Eben Byer...
    C. ...radium; Eben Byer...
    D. ...radium; however, Eben Byer...
    E. ...radium, then Eben Byer...

4. Of the following choices, which is the least likely to rouse the author's skepticism?
    A. global positioning systems in automobiles
    B. synthetic sweeteners
    C. organic produce
    D. weight-loss supplements
    E. tooth-whitening strips

Review

Lessons 7 – 9

EXERCISE I – Inferences

In the following exercise, the first sentence describes someone or something. Infer information from the first sentence, and then choose the word from the Word Bank that best completes the second sentence.

Word Bank

painstaking	immaterial	innate	dainty
integral	detriment	solace	insubordinate

1. The baby deer scrambled to its feet in the minutes following its birth.
   From this sentence, we can infer that the deer's ability to walk is _____.

2. If the rocket boosters are not fired in time, the spaceship will burn up in the atmosphere.
   From this sentence, we can infer that firing the rocket motors is _____ to the survival of the spaceship.

3. Before the flood, dozens of volunteers braved cold, pouring rain and knee-deep mud to fill sandbags to stack along the riverbanks.
   From this sentence, we can infer that flood preparations were _____ work.

4. Vince lost his job when he refused to follow his boss's instructions.
   From this sentence, we can infer that Vince was _____ at work.

5. Kylie's term paper was full of errors because she wrote it while trying to watch television.
   From this sentence, we can infer that television was a[n] _____ to Kylie's writing ability.

EXERCISE II – Related Words

Some of the vocabulary words from lessons 7–9 have related meanings. Complete the following sentences by choosing the word that best completes the specified relationship. Some word pairs will be antonyms, some will be synonyms, and some will be words often used in the same context.

1. A *mentor* has a purpose opposite to that of a[n]
    A. octogenarian.
    B. jurisdiction.
    C. genre.
    D. zenith.
    E. antagonist.

2. The word *sanctuary* is most synonymous with
    A. jurisdiction.
    B. haven.
    C. drudgery.
    D. pantheon.
    E. solace.

3. If you *impugn* someone in a statement, and then you find out that you were wrong, you might _____ your statement.
    A. badger
    B. implore
    C. retract
    D. permeate
    E. tether

4. If a project is described as *drudgery*, then it might involve work that is
    A. dainty.
    B. painstaking.
    C. fitful.
    D. innate.
    E. benevolent.

5. *Solace* contrasts most with the word
    A. alight.
    B. elapse.
    C. kindle.
    D. wince.
    E. badger.

6. A wild animal might become *listless* if it has a[n] _____ food supply.
    A. meager
    B. immaterial
    C. dainty
    D. vertical
    E. integral

7. The *insubordinate* worker's feelings for his supervisor were not
    A. innate.
    B. detriments.
    C. benevolent.
    D. somber.
    E. fitful.

8. The wood will soon be *alight* if someone _____ it properly.
    A. kindles
    B. convalesces
    C. tethers
    D. sears
    E. badgers

9. The opposite of the word *integral* is the word
    A. benevolent.
    B. horizontal.
    C. insubordinate.
    D. immaterial.
    E. innate.

10. One person's *feint* may cause his or her opponent to
    A. tether.
    B. wince.
    C. implore.
    D. impugn.
    E. alight.

EXERCISE III – Crossword Puzzle

Use the clues to complete the crossword puzzle. The answers consist of vocabulary words from lessons 7 through 9.

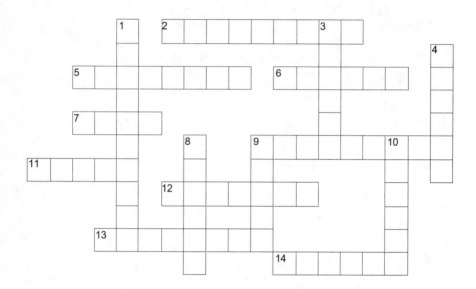

Across

2. The _____ criticized my unhealthy diet just before he ate four chocolate doughnuts for breakfast.
5. The staff of the university was a[n] _____ of world-renown scholars.
6. Laura had nightmares during her _____ sleep.
7. The blast from the rocket motor will _____ the concrete pad and the surrounding grass.
9. The back injury proved to be a[n] _____ to her comfort for years to come.
11. The author combined two _____[s] when she wrote a mystery novel set in outer space.
12. The child _____[ed] his mother for just one more cookie.
13. You should change your clothes if the gasoline fumes _____ them.

14. People can get hurt if they _____ with the electrical wiring of their homes.

Down

1. It took Quentin two weeks to _____ from his bout with pneumonia.
3. She had to _____ her dog to a bicycle rack before she could walk into the pharmacy.
4. At noon, the sun is at its _____.
8. The _____ music was appropriate for the depressing movie scene.
9. The fire whistle _____[s] for five minutes during the weekly system test.
10. Three hours must _____ before the paint will be dry.

Lesson Ten

1. **brash** (brash) *adj.* hasty in thought; offensively bold
Carl is usually very polite, so his *brash* tone of voice surprised everyone.
syn: rash; careless   *ant: polite; thoughtful*

2. **buff** (buf) *n.* an enthusiast
                    v. to polish with soft material
(n) The movie *buff* could quote lines from hundreds of old films.
(v) When you finish waxing the car, please *buff* it until it shines.
(n) *syn: fan; aficionado*   *ant: beginner; dabbler*

3. **intemperate** (in tem´ pər it) *adj.* excessive in behavior; unrestrained
One *intemperate* remark during the interview cost the applicant the job.

4. **interrogate** (in ter´ ə gāt) *v.* to question formally
The detective *interrogated* the suspect until he was sure that the man was
innocent.
syn: grill; quiz

5. **moot** (mōōt) *adj.* subject to debate; disputable; doubtful
The teacher began each class by making a *moot* statement about a sensitive topic.
syn: debatable; controversial   *ant: established; recognized*

6. **opaque** (ō pāk´) *adj.* impenetrable by light; not transparent or
       translucent
The *opaque* curtains in the bedroom block the bright morning sun.
syn: solid   *ant: transparent; clear; see-through*

7. **pragmatic** (prag mat´ ik) *adj.* practical; concerned with facts and
       observation rather than theory
When working on an engine, the *pragmatic* mechanic first eliminates the
simplest causes of malfunction before opening manuals or disassembling
the whole car.
syn: realistic; logical   *ant: idealistic*

8. **prestigious** (pre stē´ jəs) *adj.* esteemed widely; distinguished
I once received a *prestigious* award for my essay on politics.
syn: prominent; celebrated   *ant: unknown; obscure*

9. **prodigy** (prod´ ə jē) *n.* a person with extraordinary ability or talent
The musical *prodigy* composed his first symphony at the age of ten.
syn: genius

10. **savory** (sā´ və rē) *adj.*   1. appetizing
     2. pleasingly respectable
     (1) The fast food looked *savory* in the advertisement, but it looked unappealing at the restaurant.
     (2) To be an FBI agent, you must have a *savory* background that shows you can be trusted.
     (1) *syn: flavorful; tasty*   *ant: unpalatable*
     (2) *syn: acceptable; wholesome*   *ant: objectionable; distasteful*

11. **sedate** (si dāt´) *v.* to tranquilize; to calm   *adj.*   calm and reserved
     (v)   The veterinarian *sedated* the dog before the operation.
     (adj) The *sedate* colonel did not even blink as enemy bombs exploded around the bunker.
     (v)   *syn: anesthetize*   *ant: stimulate; excite*
     (adj) *syn: staid; demure*   *ant: boisterous; unruly*

12. **singular** (sing´ gyə lər) *adj.*   exceptional; distinguished from others
     Management honored the *singular* worker with a raise in salary.
     syn: unique; uncommon   *ant: ordinary; average*

13. **spontaneous** (spon tā´ nē əs) *adj.*   unplanned
     The family took a *spontaneous* trip to the state park for a hike and a picnic.
     syn: impulsive; impromptu; improvisational   *ant: premeditated; planned*

14. **usurp** (ū sûrp´) *v.*   to take over illegally; to seize by force without right
     Macbeth *usurped* the throne by murdering King Duncan.
     syn: commandeer; grab   *ant: surrender; relinquish*

15. **whimsical** (wim´ si kəl) *adj.*   playful; fanciful
     Many children's books feature *whimsical* characters.
     syn: capricious; droll   *ant: solemn; grim*

EXERCISE I – Words in Context

Using the vocabulary list for this lesson, supply the correct word to complete each sentence.

1. The doctor _____ the hysterical patient who witnessed the traumatic event.

2. The rebels _____ the captured spy until they got the information they needed.

3. Only the brightest students gain entrance to the _____ university.

4. So that no one would be alerted to their presence in the abandoned house, the thieves covered all the windows with a[n] _____ film.

5. Johnny's _____ remark to his teacher bought him a week of detention.

6. Tracey likes very organized vacations, but Ben prefers _____ activities that require no planning.

7. The restaurant was famous for its _____ cuisine.

8. Kim painted _____ cartoon animals and shapes on the walls of the nursery.

9. The leader of the revolution _____ control from the king and ruled the country for three years.

10. The drill sergeant ordered the recruits to _____ the floor until it sparkled.

11. The poor service is the _____ reason why I do not go to that restaurant.

12. Her point is _____ because she's not even sure that it's true.

13. The _____ graduated from high school at the age of fourteen.

14. The _____ detective does not allow his personal opinions to interfere with his investigations.

15. His _____ lifestyle caught up with him when he was arrested for driving while intoxicated.

EXERCISE II – Sentence Completion

Complete the sentence in a way that shows you understand the meaning of the italicized vocabulary word.

1. Contestants on the game show tried to *usurp* the title from...

2. The Collector's Outlet is the *singular* store for people who...

3. After years of hard work, Debbie was promoted to the *prestigious* position of...

4. Mentioning the *moot* subject in a public place never fails to...

5. When someone disturbs the *intemperate* neighbor's sleep, the neighbor...

6. The *sedate* pilot did not panic when...

7. The chef uses a *savory* mixture of herbs and spices to...

8. Her *spontaneous* outburst in the restaurant caused...

9. Since the windows were *opaque*, no one could...

10. The airport security guards *interrogate* anyone who...

11. The grandfather told the child a *whimsical* story about...

12. Sam is a comic book *buff*, so he...

13. The math *prodigy* has the ability to...

14. The *pragmatic* man liked practical gifts more than...

15. If you make a *brash* decision now, you might...

EXERCISE III – Prefixes and Suffixes

Study the entries and use them to complete the questions that follow.

The suffix -*ation* means "act of" or "result of."
The suffix -*er* means "one who does."
The suffix -*ious* means "full of."
The suffix -*ism* means "system" or "system of."

Use the provided prefixes and suffixes to change each word so that it completes the sentence correctly. Then, keeping in mind that prefixes and suffixes sometimes change the part of speech, identify the part of speech of the new word by circling N for a noun, V for a verb, or ADJ for an adjective.

1. (pragmatic) Though she is always ready to hear new ideas, the boss encourages _____ because the best solution is often the simple, practical one.　　　　　　　　　　　　N　　V　　ADJ

2. (usurp) Critics of the new law viewed it as a[n] _____ of their constitutional rights.　　　　　　　　　N　　V　　ADJ

3. (prodigy) The _____ composer wrote three symphonies in a single year.　　　　　　　　　　　　N　　V　　ADJ

4. (usurp) The king worried that a[n] _____ was plotting to remove him from power and take the throne.
　　　　　　　　　　　　　　　　N　　V　　ADJ

EXERCISE IV – Critical Reading

The following reading passage contains vocabulary words from this lesson. Carefully read the passage and then choose the best answers for each of the questions that follow.

Imagine for a moment that you are 43,000 years old. When you were born, the first *homo sapiens* (the type of humans who walk the earth today) were just replacing their more primitive ancestors. You were already about 38,000 when humans invented writing; by the time they
5   got to the moon, you were 42,969.

A century is just another day for *Lomatia Tasmania*, or King's Holly, the world's oldest plant. This plant and the few others that have managed to reach record-breaking ages form a **singular** and fascinating group.

While mining in 1937, a talented nature **buff** named Deny King dis-
10   covered what he thought might be a new species of plant growing the wild lands of Tasmania. The plant was named for King, and scientists eventually noticed that there was something different about King's Holly. Fossilized leaves found near the plant were genetically identical to the live plant—but they were 43,000 years old! This means the current plant is
15   actually a *clone*—essentially the same organism as that which produced the ancient fossil leaves. Further research revealed the reason for the similarity: *Lomatia Tasmania* does not bear fruit or seeds. In fact, a rare chromosome mutation makes the holly unable to produce sexually (that is, by means of fruit and seeds). Instead, it must reproduce vegetatively,
20   dropping root suckers that eventually grow into new clones of the original plant.

In the world of ancient plants that clone themselves, the King's Holly has some competition. The creosote bush of California's Mojave Desert is a runner-up. Circles of this shrub grow over a wide range of the desert.
25   Each member of the circle is genetically identical to the others; when a single growth of creosote matures, it splits into fragments, which then grow outward to make the bush circular in shape. The center of the wood dies, but the outer portion of the circle lives on, producing new branches. One 50-foot ring of shrubs has been dated back 12,000 years!

30   The oldest non-cloned tree is a bristlecone pine (nicknamed "Methuselah," after a man of legendary age mentioned in the Old Testament) growing in California's Inyo National Forest. It has managed to survive for 5,000 years in one of the most **intemperate** environments on the planet. At its high elevation (about 10,000 feet above sea level),
35   heavy winds blow almost constantly, and nutrients and water are scarce. The tree has not only adapted to these conditions; it has learned to take advantage of them. It has evolved a wide crown and root system to draw

moisture from a greater area, its bark is highly resistant to disease, and it
can go dormant during **spontaneous** drought. It is specifically this last
40 ability that has seen it through the toughest times; much as animals simply avoid the harshest winter conditions by hibernating, Methuselah can
"sleep off" a whole series of bad years.

   These incredible plants are distinguished by one thing: stability. They
remain the same—genetically, environmentally, physically—for hundreds,
45 then thousands, of years. Few predators disturb them; few diseases affect
them; few or no changes are made to their genetic code. If the environment changes radically, however, the plants may have difficulty surviving;
King's Holly, for instance, has begun to die off because of diseases brought
by human foot traffic, and is now classified as endangered. If it does lose
50 its battle, we will lose a remarkable treasure: one of the few living records
of the whole history of life.

1. How are the living leaves of King's Holly related to the plant's fossil
    leaves?
    A. The living leaves are descendants of the plant on which the fossil
        leaves once grew.
    B. They are genetically the same, and therefore count as one individual.
    C. They are unrelated; the fossil leaves are from an extinct species of
        King's Holly.
    D. They are genetically similar and grouped in the same family of
        organisms.
    E. The living leaves sprouted from the fossilized leaves thousands of
        years ago.

2. As used in line 9, the word *buff* most nearly means
    A. devotee.
    B. addict.
    C. shine.
    D. scientist.
    E. enthusiasm.

3. "Methuselah" is unlike the creosote bush and King's Holly in that it is
    A. resistant to disease.
    B. found in desert climates only.
    C. unusually unstable.
    D. 43,000 years old.
    E. not a clone.

4. As used in line 39, the word *spontaneous* most nearly means
   A. rapid.
   B. unnatural.
   C. unexpected.
   D. devastating.
   E. surprising.

5. This passage is best described as
   A. an argumentative essay about global warming.
   B. an analytical essay about plants that clone themselves.
   C. a compare/contrast essay about plant environments.
   D. a narrative essay about the discovery of ancient organisms.
   E. an informative essay about the oldest plants on Earth.

Lesson Eleven

1. **authoritarian** (ə thôr i târ´ ē ən) *adj.* pertaining to absolute authority
      and unquestioning obedience
   The *authoritarian* boss seldom allows his workers to make their own decisions.
   syn: totalitarian   *ant: democratic*

2. **avenge** (ə venj´) *v.* to inflict punishment for a perceived wrong; to
      take vengeance
   Monty decided to *avenge* the insult by hitting Derek with a water balloon.
   syn: retaliate; payback   *ant: tolerate; forgive*

3. **bewilder** (bē wil´ dər) *v.* to confuse
   The home team's loss *bewildered* fans who expected to have a winning
   season.
   syn: baffle; perplex   *ant: clarify; simplify*

4. **bristle** (bris´ əl) *v.* to become angry
   The radio host's insult made many listeners *bristle*.
   syn: fume; infuriate   *ant: calm; relax*

5. **clemency** (klem´ ən sē) *n.* mercy; leniency
   The strict teacher has no *clemency* for students who cut class and then
   fail their tests.
   syn: forgiveness; compassion   *ant: strictness; sternness*

6. **elaborate** (i lab´ ə rāt) *v.* to express in greater detail
                (i lab´ ə rit) *adj.* having intricate or complex detail
   (v)   The students appeared to be puzzled, so the teacher *elaborated* on
         the topic.
   (adj) The rooms of the Victorian house featured *elaborate*, hand-carved
         woodwork.
   (v)   *syn: expound; clarify*   *ant: simplify; condense*
   (adj) *syn: extensive; thorough*   *ant: simple; plain*

7. **gazebo** (gə zē´ bō) *n.* a small, roofed building, usually having open
      sides
   The small orchestra played a concert in the *gazebo* at the park.

8. **malady** (mal´ ə dē) *n.* an illness; a physical or mental disorder
   Measles was a common *malady* before vaccinations existed.
   syn: sickness; disease   *ant: wellness; healthiness; vigor*

9. **mar** (mär) *v.*   to damage; to disfigure
    Water leaking from the roof *marred* the wallpaper.
    syn: ruin; impair   *ant: beautify; improve*

10. **obscure** (ob skyŏŏr´) *adj.*   1. not easily noticed or understood
                                              2. little known
                                        v.   to make unclear; to dim
    (a.1) It was an *obscure* ritual to outsiders but an ancient tradition to the
          natives.
    (a.2) Milton excels at trivia games because he knows so many *obscure*
          facts.
    (v)   The poor translation *obscures* the meaning of the original text.
    (a.1) *syn: unclear; ambiguous*   *ant: obvious*
    (a.2) *syn: mysterious; esoteric*   *ant: famous; popular*
    (v)   *syn: mask; cloak; shroud*   *ant: reveal; disclose; clarify*

11. **obsolete** (ob sə lēt´) *adj.*   no longer valid or in use
    The *obsolete* computer at the library does not run any modern programs.
    syn: outdated; archaic   *ant: modern; new*

12. **pretext** (prē´ tekst) *n.*   a professed purpose to hide the real reason
    Liz kept the wallet she found with the *pretext* of keeping it safe until she
    could locate the owner.
    syn: excuse; alibi; reason

13. **teem** (tēm) *v.*   1. to be full of things
                            2. to move in large numbers; to pour out
    (1) The fisherman's net was heavy because it *teemed* with fish.
    (2) Eager fans *teemed* into the concert hall, leaving standing room only.
    (1) *syn: abound; overflow*   *ant: lack*
    (2) *syn: empty; stream*   *ant: trickle*

14. **translucent** (trans lōō´ sənt) *adj.*   permitting light to pass through, but
    not enough to allow clear viewing of objects on the other side
    The *translucent* glass in the bathroom windows provides some privacy but
    allows light to enter the room.
    syn: clouded

15. **transparent** (trans pâr´ ənt) *adj.*   permitting enough light to pass
        through to allow clear viewing of objects on the other side
    The pen is *transparent* so the writer can see how much ink remains.
    syn: clear; see-through   *ant: opaque*

EXERCISE I – Words in Context

Using the vocabulary list for this lesson, supply the correct word to complete each sentence.

1. He vowed to _____ the death of his friend by finding the killer.

2. She was confident in the worker's skills, so she did not _____ on her simple instructions.

3. The _____ rules of the military academy dissuade some students from applying for admission.

4. Company shareholders _____ when an executive's mistake caused them to lose fortunes because of sharply declining stock values.

5. Poison ivy exposure is a common _____ for campers.

6. Gayle could see only vague figures passing behind the _____, stained-glass windows.

7. The fire might not consume the house, but the smoke will _____ everything inside.

8. A fence outside the window _____ our view of the river.

9. The policeman used a routine traffic stop as a[n] _____ to search the suspicious vehicle.

10. Swimmers could see the ocean floor through the _____ water.

11. The comic book store _____ with collectors during the annual half-price sale.

12. The judge showed no _____ for the career criminal who had ruined so many people's lives.

13. The company replaced its _____ equipment with state-of-the-art machines.

14. Bridget built a[n] _____ in the back yard where she could sit and enjoy her garden.

15. Mike's failing grade on the test _____ him because he thought he had done very well.

EXERCISE II – Sentence Completion

Complete the sentence in a way that shows you understand the meaning of the italicized vocabulary word.

1. The warrior swore he would *avenge* his brother's death by...

2. Certain *maladies* can be avoided by...

3. Few people remembered the *elaborate* rules of the game, so they...

4. He went to the foreign nation under the *pretext* of business, but he really planned to...

5. Because the bottle is made of *translucent* glass, you can...

6. The natives' *obsolete* weapons were no match for...

7. Josh thought that he was home alone, so he was *bewildered* when he...

8. Emma *bristled* when her parents...

9. Some *obscure* authors become famous when...

10. The old house *teemed* with termites, so the owner decided...

11. Instead of showing *clemency* to the inferior home team, the visiting team...

12. The boat has a *transparent* bottom so passengers can...

13. If the heat *mars* the chocolates, no one will...

14. On Independence Day, people crowd around the *gazebo* in the park to watch...

15. *Authoritarian* leadership is necessary when...

EXERCISE III – Prefixes and Suffixes

Study the entries and use them to complete the questions that follow.

The suffix -*ism* means "system" or "system of."
The suffix -*ity* means "state of" or "quality of."
The suffix -*ment* means "result of."
The suffix -*ness* means "state," "quality," or "condition."

Use the provided prefixes and suffixes to change each word so that it completes the sentence correctly. Then, keeping in mind that prefixes and suffixes sometimes change the part of speech, identify the part of speech of the new word by circling N for a noun, V for a verb, or ADJ for an adjective.

1. (obscure) Having squandered his fortune and alienated his friends, the once-famous writer died in _____.

    N   V   ADJ

2. (elaborate) The _____ of the hand-carved furniture and woodwork inside the mansion amazed most visitors.

    N   V   ADJ

3. (authoritarian) Students and teachers alike began to question the new principal's _____ when he enforced one-way traffic in certain school hallways.   N   V   ADJ

4. (obscure) The _____ of earth's atmosphere limits what we can see in space through telescopes.   N   V   ADJ

EXERCISE IV – Critical Reading

The following reading passage contains vocabulary words from this lesson. Carefully read the passage and then choose the best answers for each of the questions that follow.

1   Before he invented the hobbit, or teamed dwarves, elves, and humans to battle evil wizards, John Ronald Reuel (J.R.R.) Tolkien excelled in the study of languages, especially **obsolete** languages such as Greek and Latin, and the **obscure** tongues of Gothic, Welsh, and Finnish. This was also a study of history, for the characteristics and evolution of a language reflect the history and beliefs of its users. Some of the languages Tolkien studied exist primarily as poems and sagas of bygone cultures. Some of those tales, notably Icelandic sagas, chronicle high adventures in which mankind confronts its greatest fears, and sometimes those fears take the form of imaginary creatures such as trolls, dwarves, elves, and orcs—all major players in Tolkien's masterworks, *The Hobbit* and *The Lord of the Rings.*

2   We can thank Norse mythology for trolls. Folklore trolls range from small children to the giants in Tolkien's fictional realm. They usually have human features, though their noses, ears, and teeth are greatly exaggerated. Like many monsters in Viking legend, trolls inhabit dark forests, mountains, or caves, and sometimes they commit the standard monster-atrocities such as stealing children or, as the popular nursery tale *The Three Billy Goats Gruff* warns, devouring livestock.

3   Dwarves are also creatures of Scandinavian folklore. These little people, usually three- to four-feet tall, are said to dwell underground where they mine tin and precious metals and hoard vast treasures. Dwarves of myth, such as Tolkien portrays, are excellent miners and masterly smiths capable of fabricating the finest armor. They are not especially pleasing to the eye, they **bristle** easily if provoked, and they are said to live much longer than humans, perhaps hundreds of years, like elves.

4   Elves are originally from Germanic myth, though they eventually spread to northern Europe. Close to humans in appearance except, of course, for their pointy ears and tiny stature, elves were thought to be of an immortal race having magical powers. Early elves, like other sprites and faeries, liked to **bewilder** humans with playful pranks, but in legend, the elves grew to be the man-sized, reclusive, magical mortals portrayed in Tolkien's world.

5   Tolkien's orcs (goblins, in *The Hobbit*) are fiendish, manlike creatures from the underworld, and quite appropriately so: in Roman mythology, *Orcus* is synonymous with the name *Pluto*, the god of the underworld. Tolkien obviously took a few liberties in creating his orcs, but their general image as evil, subhuman creatures had been established centuries before.

6   Middle Earth (the **elaborate**, fictional setting of *The Hobbit* and *The Lord of the Rings*) might **teem** with borrowed legends, but Tolkien himself invented the hobbit, the jovial inhabitant of the Shire who single-handedly inspired a whole new genre of fiction. The hobbit first appeared when Tolkien half-heartedly scribbled the line, "In a hole in the ground there lived a hobbit." Hobbits soon populated the bedtime stories that Tolkien told his four children, and, in 1937, *The Hobbit* became the first modern fantasy novel in print. Perhaps, thousands of years ago, elves, dwarves, and orcs made their debut in bedtime stories, too.

1.   Which choice best paraphrases the following phrase from paragraph 1?

> ...the characteristics and evolution of a language
> reflect the history and beliefs of its users.

    A. Language is a record of history.
    B. Language inspires history.
    C. Language is a written record of a culture's history and beliefs.
    D. History would not exist without language to record it.
    E. History is vital to language.

2.   As used in paragraph 3, *bristle* most nearly means
    A. fight.
    B. argue.
    C. stun.
    D. irritate.
    E. anger.

3.   According to the passage, the hobbit originated in
    A. Tolkien's studies of Icelandic sagas.
    B. Germanic mythology.
    C. Finnish legend.
    D. Tolkien's imagination.
    E. Greek and Latin roots.

4.   As used in paragraph 4, *bewilder* most nearly means
    A. anger.
    B. confuse.
    C. bother.
    D. aggravate.
    E. frustrate.

5. The author wrote this passage to
   A. refute suggestions that Tolkien had no original ideas.
   B. explain the origins of characters in Tolkien's fiction.
   C. explain the importance of studying language.
   D. analyze the role of monsters in folklore.
   E. discuss how Icelandic sagas influenced Tolkien.

Lesson Twelve

1. **appall** (ə pôl´) *v.* to fill with horror, disgust, or outrage; to shock
    The man's terrible crime *appalled* his friends and family.
    syn: astound; horrify   *ant: comfort; reassure*

2. **constraint** (kən strānt´) *n.* something that restricts or limits
    Nick's moral *constraints* kept him out of trouble while he lived in the bad
    neighborhood.
    syn: restraint; restriction   *ant: liberty; independence*

3. **dissuade** (dis wād´) *v.* to advise against; to persuade someone out of a
        course of action
    Firemen tried to *dissuade* the man from running back into the inferno to
    rescue his cat.
    syn: discourage; deter   *ant: encourage; inspire*

4. **falter** (fôl´ tər) *v.* to hesitate; to waver
    The operation would be risky, but Tom did not *falter* in his decision to
    go through with it.
    syn: sway; delay; stumble   *ant: persist; maintain; endure*

5. **frail** (frāl) *adj.* easily broken; delicate
    The deadly disease can cause even strong young adults to become *frail*.
    syn: fragile; breakable   *ant: strong; robust*

6. **hypothetical** (hī pə thet´ i kəl) *adj.* assumed without proof; uncertain
    Ted has the *hypothetical* notion that alien life exists on Mars.
    syn: supposed; theoretical   *ant: actual; real*

7. **irate** (ī rāt´) *adj.* extremely angry; enraged
    The *irate* customer was so upset that she could not speak.
    syn: furious; fuming   *ant: delighted; happy*

8. **peninsula** (pə nin´ sə lə) *n.* a piece of land that extends from the
        mainland into a body of water
    The *peninsula* was susceptible to flooding during tropical storms.

9. **placid** (plas´ id) *adj.* calm; peaceful
    Fishing on the *placid* lake is a great way to relax.
    syn: tranquil; serene   *ant: turbulent; riotous*

10. **prejudice** (prej´ ə dis) *n.* 1. an opinion formed without knowledge of the facts
    2. an irrational suspicion or hostility toward a particular group, race, or religion
    (1) You will enjoy the movie if you watch it without *prejudice*.
    (2) She has *prejudice* against them even though she has never met them.
    (1) *syn: bias; predisposition*
    (2) *syn: bigotry; discrimination*   *ant: fairness; neutrality*

11. **prelude** (prā´ lōōd) *n.* an introductory event, action, or performance
    Discovering that the roof leaks was merely a *prelude* to the many problems Joe would find in his new house.
    syn: beginning; preface   *ant: finale; ending*

12. **profane** (prō fān´) *adj.* showing contempt for what is sacred; disrespectful to religion; vulgar
    Tammy scolded Billy for using such *profane* language.
    syn: irreverent; wicked   *ant: pious; virtuous*

13. **puny** (pyōō´ nē) *adj.* less than normal in size and strength
    Our garden tomatoes were *puny* this year because of the drought.
    syn: undersized; small   *ant: robust; sturdy*

14. **ruthless** (rōōth´ lis) *adj.* without compassion or mercy; harsh
    The *ruthless* executive tolerated neither mistakes nor excuses.
    syn: callous; merciless   *ant: merciful; compassionate; lenient*

15. **skirmish** (skûr´ mish) *n.* a minor, short-lived battle
    Many *skirmishes* took place near the border before someone finally declared war.
    syn: clash; scuffle   *ant: campaign; crusade*

EXERCISE I – Words in Context

Using the vocabulary list for this lesson, supply the correct word to complete each sentence.

1. After enjoying a[n] _____ weekend at the cabin, Malcolm was ready to return to his hectic job.

2. If you _____ in your answer, they might think you are not telling the truth.

3. The defendant's outrageous behavior in the courtroom _____ everyone present.

4. Jamie is allowed to use the car, but with the _____ that she always return it with a full tank of gas.

5. The tugboat looks _____ compared to the battleship, but the little boat has no difficulty towing the enormous ship.

6. As a[n] _____ to the Independence Day celebration, the city hosted a parade.

7. Brad tried to _____ his elderly father from going skydiving.

8. His use of _____ language in the restaurant made the other customers uncomfortable.

9. Other than a[n] _____ over some seats in the front row, the concert was peaceful.

10. She did not abandon her _____ against people of the foreign nation until she learned that she shared many of their beliefs and customs.

11. Having a reputation as a ferocious warrior, the _____ commander took no prisoners in battle.

12. Because it is more than 3,000 years old, the _____ vase cannot be touched without risk of its shattering.

13. Since it is surrounded by water on three sides, the _____ is a good place for fishing or simply watching the sunrise.

14. Aaron becomes _____ when telemarketers call his house while he is eating dinner.

15. Astronomers have constructed only _____ models of the universe because no one knows what it really looks like.

EXERCISE II – Sentence Completion

Complete the sentence in a way that shows you understand the meaning of the italicized vocabulary word.

1. Justin's *prejudice* prevented him from…

2. The actress *faltered* on stage when…

3. Brandon's mom was *appalled* to see…

4. The *placid* setting of the resort is perfect for…

5. A *skirmish* resulted when…

6. When the driver made a *profane* gesture, the police officer…

7. One *constraint* in owing the historic house is that the owner is not allowed to…

8. To get food, the *puny* dog had to…

9. The *ruthless* villain was willing to…

10. The boss tried to *dissuade* the employee from quitting by…

11. As a *prelude* to the grand opening of the new store, the mayor…

12. When Ryan touched the *frail* artifact, it…

13. A lighthouse on the *peninsula* signaled…

14. If you are *irate* about something your friend did, then you should…

15. Nicole used a *hypothetical* situation as an example to…

EXERCISE III – Prefixes and Suffixes

Study the entries and use them to complete the questions that follow.

The prefix *per-* means "completely" or "through."
The suffix *-ar* means "pertaining to."
The suffix *-ive* means "tending to."
The suffix *-ness* means "state," "quality," or "condition."

Use the provided prefixes and suffixes to change each word so that it completes the sentence correctly. Then, keeping in mind that prefixes and suffixes sometimes change the part of speech, identify the part of speech of the new word by circling N for a noun, V for a verb, or ADJ for an adjective.

1. (dissuade) Seeing the damage from a hurricane might be _____ to someone who is considering buying beach-front property.

    N   V   ADJ

2. (ruthless) Few citizens escape the _____ of the dictator.

    N   V   ADJ

3. (dissuade) A good salesperson will _____ customers to continue buying his or her products.   N   V   ADJ

4. (peninsula) The _____ state borders the ocean on three sides.

    N   V   ADJ

EXERCISE IV – Improving Paragraphs

Read the following passage and then answer the multiple-choice questions that follow. The questions will require you to make decisions regarding the revision of the reading selection.

(1) Take a look at your #2 pencil; that is, if you have not abandoned it for a mechanical pencil. (2) Excluding the eraser, the #2 pencil is made of two materials: wood and graphite. (3) It has no moving parts. (4) It is long lasting, but the **frail** point must be sharpened constantly. (5) Indeed, the pencil is primitive in this age of wireless links, touch-screen monitors, and MP3 players. (6) Just how old is this invention? (7) Why do we still use it when there are better alternatives? (8) And just how do they stuff that lead into the wood, anyway?

(9) The answers began in Egypt, 4,000 years ago. (10) Some time between pyramid-building and mummy-making, Egyptians learned that they could make paper, or *papyrus*, out of big weeds that grow along the Nile River banks. (11) Egyptians used pieces of lead or other soft minerals to write notes on this early personal stationery.

(12) Papyrus and lead eventually made it to the ancient Romans, who prided themselves on their many advancements and high quality of life. (13) Because they knew the importance of being *seen* writing, they had already invented the *stylus*, a pen-sized, sometimes ornate, sharp metal stick, to carve letters into wax tablets. (14) Styli made of lead were tried by Romans to write on paper, but the **puny** sticks left only faint marks, so writers switched to lead discs that could withstand greater writing pressure. (15) To create their most important documents, Romans painted words with a *pencillus,* or small brush.

(16) When the Roman Empire **faltered** and collapsed, so did advancement of the pencil. (17) The quill eventually replaced the pencillus in a **prelude** to the modern pen, but not until the sixteenth century did the pencil experience a major change. (17) That is when the English discovered an extremely rare deposit of graphite, or pure carbon, in northwest England's Cumbria region.

(18) The graphite was so pure and solid that it could be sawed off in sheets and cut into sticks. (19) It immediately proved useful in pencils, and soon artists were carving square handles out of wood to hold the graphite rods, or *leads* (discoverers assumed erroneously that carbon was simply a form of lead). (20) The first pencils made by artists were rectangular, not cylindrical.

(21) England held a monopoly on graphite pencils until 1662, when Germans found that mixing graphite powder (separated from impure ore) with lead and antimony made it solid enough to use in pencils. (22) It worked, but not nearly as well as the pure graphite. (23) England enjoyed its monopoly for another century.

(24) During the French Revolutionary Wars (1792-1801), England blocked the export of graphite, leaving Napoleon with no way to write **ruthless** military

strategies or complete his favorite crossword puzzles. (25) French scientist Nicholas-Jacques Conte solved the problem in 1795 by adding clay to graphite powder and then firing the mixture in a kiln. (26) The pencils were superb, and adjusting the hardness of the lead was a simple matter of changing the amount of clay in the mixture. (27) Conte had invented the modern pencil.

(28) The pencil has been perfected further since 1795, but its design and materials are essentially unchanged. (29) Pencil manufacturing, on the other hand, has certainly changed. (30) No, no one sits in a factory all day and drills holes in pencils; the wooden handle of a pencil is, in fact, two halves glued together after the lead is set in place. (31) A nice paint job hides the seam.

(32) Who knows what the future has in store for the pencil?

1. The underlined portion of sentence 14 is best improved by which revision?

> Styli made of lead were tried by Romans to write on paper, but the **puny** sticks left only faint marks, so writers switched to lead discs that could withstand greater writing pressure.

    A. Romans did not try to write on paper with lead,
    B. A lead stylus does not write on paper,
    C. The lead did not work well on paper,
    D. Lead styli were too soft to use on paper by the Romans,
    E. Romans tried using lead styli on paper,

2. Which choice best describes the problem with sentence 20?
    A. pronoun disagreement
    B. redundant information
    C. incorrect verb *made*
    D. *artists* should be capitalized
    E. lacks proper punctuation

3. If inserted to follow sentence 32, which sentence would improve the conclusion of the passage?
    A. This hereby concludes an essay about the history of the pencil.
    B. Soon, personal spacecraft will transport us to vacations on the moons of Saturn, but we will still need pencils for postcards!
    C. It is hard to tell, but since it took 4,000 years for the pencil to get to this point, do not expect anything to happen soon.
    D. Only modern pencil-makers and their shareholders have the answer.
    E. Who cares?

4.	The author poses questions in the passage, but this technique is not fulfilled because
	A.	the tone of the passage is too casual for an academic paper.
	B.	the passage does not sufficiently cover the development of pens.
	C.	the passage is too lengthy for such a simple topic.
	D.	the subject of the essay is unrelated to the subject of the questions.
	E.	the passage fails to answer one of the three questions in the introduction.

Review

Lessons 10 – 12

EXERCISE I – Inferences

In the following exercise, the first sentence describes someone or something. Infer information from the first sentence, and then choose the word from the Word Bank that best completes the second sentence.

Word Bank

prestigious	pragmatic	spontaneous	obsolete
authoritarian	frail	placid	hypothetical

1. Thomas based his decision not on what might happen, but on what has actually happened.
   From this sentence, we can infer that Tom is _____.

2. The crystals must be kept in an airtight room, because even a small breeze is strong enough to topple the new formations.
   From this sentence, we can infer that the crystals are _____.

3. According to the engineers, the new microprocessor design should be thousands of times faster than traditional designs, but no one has built one yet.
   From this sentence, we can infer that the new microprocessor's performance is _____.

4. Without any planning, Steve grabbed his fishing pole and spent the whole day at the river.
   From this sentence, we can infer that Steve made a[n] _____ decision to go fishing.

5. During boot camp, drill instructors tell recruits when to eat, when to sleep, how to dress, and how to speak; those who cannot obey are dropped from training.
   From this sentence, we can infer that drill instructors are _____ leaders.

EXERCISE II – Related Words

Some of the vocabulary words from lessons 10–12 have related meanings. Complete the following sentences by choosing the word that best completes the specified relationship. Some word pairs will be antonyms, some will be synonyms, and some will be words often used in the same context.

1. The word *opaque* contrasts most with the word
    A. translucent.
    B. frail.
    C. transparent.
    D. obscure.
    E. moot.

2. To unwilling followers, an *authoritarian* leader might appear to be
    A. placid.
    B. pragmatic.
    C. savory.
    D. whimsical.
    E. ruthless.

3. *Sedate* most nearly means the opposite of
    A. usurp.
    B. bristle.
    C. falter.
    D. dissuade.
    E. teem.

4. *Brash* people might make _____ statements that they later regret.
    A. spontaneous
    B. savory
    C. whimsical
    D. hypothetical
    E. obsolete

5. The word *profane* contrasts most with the word
    A. ruthless.
    B. intemperate.
    C. pragmatic.
    D. savory.
    E. irate.

6. If people *interrogate* you, they might want you to _____ on your answers to their questions.
   A. bewilder
   B. mar
   C. elaborate
   D. usurp
   E. dissuade

7. An *obscure* school would probably not be
   A. prestigious.
   B. savory.
   C. puny.
   D. frail.
   E. moot.

8. An *irate* person is not likely to be
   A. profane.
   B. prestigious.
   C. brash.
   D. placid.
   E. ruthless.

9. If a young *buff* is especially talented in his or her area of interest, he or she might be said to be a[n]
   A. malady.
   B. prodigy.
   C. prejudice.
   D. gazebo.
   E. peninsula.

10. A *pragmatic* person would not make decisions based on evidence that is
    A. profane.
    B. authoritarian.
    C. prestigious.
    D. hypothetical.
    E. singular.

EXERCISE III – Crossword Puzzle

Use the clues to complete the crossword puzzle. The answers consist of vocabulary words from lessons 10 through 12.

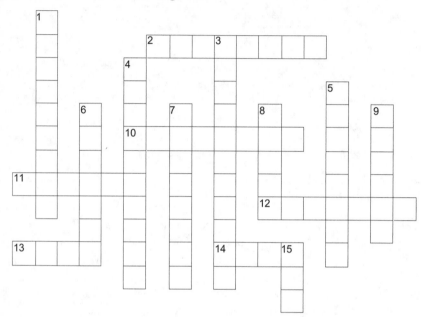

Across

2. The workers had not complained recently, so the sudden strike _____ [ed] the owner of the factory.

10. A[n] _____ broke out when the two families disagreed over the location of the property line.

11. If the bowler _____[s] during his approach, he will not throw the ball properly.

12. A delicious appetizer was served as a[n] _____ to the gourmet feast.

13. The debate was over until a new incident made the subject _____ once again.

14. The pond will _____ with fish once the food supply returns.

Down

1. During the puppet show, _____ characters learned to work together during their comical adventures.

3. The doctor said that a[n] _____ diet could lead to heart disease or diabetes.

4. Ted's apartment lease has the _____ that Ted cannot have pets.

5. The exterminator claims to be the _____ expert on insect control in the tri-state region.

6. The spy entered the country with the _____ of wanting to go sightseeing.

7. The angry customer tried to _____ people from visiting the restaurant.

8. Brian plans to _____ the manager's job by making the present manager appear responsible for a large mistake.

9. Black lung was a common _____ among early coal miners.

15. Mold will _____ the leather jacket if it is not stored in a dry place.

Lesson Thirteen

1. **bystander** (bī´ stan dər) *n.* a person present at an event but not participating in it; an onlooker
    The police asked *bystanders* to describe the man who robbed the convenience store.
    syn: spectator; witness   *ant: participant; contributor*

2. **cede** (sēd) *v.* to surrender; to give up or yield to another
    The farmer refused to *cede* any land to the state for the construction of the new highway.
    syn: abandon; transfer   *ant: protect; keep*

3. **comprehensive** (kom prē hen´ siv) *adj.* inclusive; extensive
    The chief told the officers that she wanted a *comprehensive* report of the incident no later than tomorrow.
    syn: complete; thorough   *ant: limited; selective*

4. **devout** (di vout´) *adj.* 1. devoted to religion
                                  2. sincere; earnest
    (1) The *devout* monks meditated in prayer several times a day.
    (2) Her low wages and humble lodgings proved her *devout* interest in helping others.
    (1) *syn: pious; reverent*   *ant: unholy; irreverent*
    (2) *syn: serious; heartfelt*   *ant: insincere; dishonest*

5. **flounder** (floun´ der) *v.* to move or speak clumsily and confusedly
    Logan *floundered* during his poorly-prepared presentation.
    syn: struggle

6. **foster** (fo´ stər) *v.* to promote the development or growth of; to nurture
    Schools should *foster* good citizenship as well as academics.
    syn: encourage; support   *ant: oppose; restrain*

7. **incite** (in sīt´) *v.* to provoke into action; to rouse
    Several of the rowdy fans were arrested for trying to *incite* a riot.
    syn: instigate; urge; galvanize   *ant: deter; prevent*

8. **pittance** (pit´ ns) *n.* a small amount
    The pawn broker gave Harry a *pittance* of what the watch was actually worth.
    syn: bit; trifle   *ant: abundance*

9. **precipitate** (pri sip´ i tāt) *v.* 1. to bring something about prematurely; to speed up
   2. to fall from the sky as rain, snow, or hail
   (1) The manager's rude comment *precipitated* Brenda's resignation from the company.
   (2) Moisture in the air will *precipitate* when the temperature reaches the dew point.
   (1) *syn: hasten; advance*   *ant: delay; prolong*

10. **restrictive** (ri strik´ tiv) *adj.* limiting
    After many accidents, the town imposed *restrictive* traffic laws.
    syn: restraining   *ant: encouraging; liberal*

11. **scurry** (skûr´ ē) *v.* to move lightly and rapidly
    The rabbits *scurried* across the lawn and hid beneath the front porch.
    syn: scamper; dash   *ant: trudge; plod*

12. **shrewd** (shrōōd) *adj.* sharp in business and practical affairs; cunning
    The *shrewd* investor seldom failed to make enormous profits.
    syn: clever; astute   *ant: naive; inexperienced*

13. **spew** (spyōō) *v.* to eject forcefully; to spit out in great quantity
    Lava *spewed* from the volcano.
    syn: gush; spurt   *ant: ooze*

14. **tact** (takt) *n.* sensitivity in dealing with others
    George, who has no *tact*, insisted on talking about his inheritance from the deceased as the funeral procession entered the cemetery.
    syn: discretion   *ant: carelessness*

15. **vigorous** (vig´ gər əs) *adj.* 1. strong and energetic in mind or body
    2. done with force and liveliness
    (1) Each day before work, Jerry goes to the gym for a *vigorous* workout.
    (2) The *vigorous* woodsman did not stop chopping wood until the entire tree had become a pile of logs.
    (1) *syn: aggressive; brisk*   *ant: slothful; lazy*
    (2) *syn: hearty; enthusiastic*   *ant: lethargic; sluggish*

EXERCISE I – Words in Context

Using the vocabulary list for this lesson, supply the correct word to complete each sentence.

1. It took eight hours for the scientist to present a[n] _____ explanation of her theory.

2. Donations _____ the growth of the new library.

3. Maria's inheritance was a mere _____ compared to the amount her sister received.

4. The _____ woman was seldom seen outside of church.

5. Two _____ were injured when the awning fell off the storefront.

6. When someone asked him a difficult question, Walt _____ because he did not know the answer.

7. A series of internal scandals _____ the collapse of the organization.

8. The _____ regulations in the state park are meant to protect the wildlife.

9. Milk _____ from Alicia's mouth when she glanced at the container and saw that it had expired two weeks ago.

10. It is wise to stretch before participating in any form of _____ exercise.

11. Ambassadors must have the _____ to deal with people of foreign cultures without offending them.

12. A[n] _____ businessperson can turn a lemonade stand into a booming corporation.

13. Jeff called the exterminator when he saw mice _____ across the basement floor.

14. Officials of the unstable nation feared that news of the scandal would _____ a rebellion.

15. A change in management forced Pam to _____ control of the project to someone else.

EXERCISE II – Sentence Completion

Complete the sentence in a way that shows you understand the meaning of the italicized vocabulary word.

1. Each night, the *devout* musician…

2. Constant, crashing waves *precipitated* the destruction of…

3. Joe hired a *shrewd* accountant to…

4. The team will have to *cede* victory to the challengers if…

5. Doug earned only a *pittance* of his usual salary when…

6. The *restrictive* rules in the factory are meant to…

7. Doing at least thirty minutes of *vigorous*, physical activity five times a week will…

8. When a big rat *scurried* across the floor, Jamie…

9. The depleted soil does not *foster*…

10. The teacher will provide *comprehensive* explanations of…

11. Someone who has no *tact* might…

12. The car sputtered, and its tailpipe *spewed*…

13. Bobby *incited* panic when he…

14. He *floundered* with the answer to the teacher's question because…

15. The *bystanders* crowded around to see the…

EXERCISE III – Prefixes and Suffixes

Study the entries and use them to complete the questions that follow.

The suffix *-ible* means "able to be."
The suffix *-ation* means "act of" or "result of."
The suffix *-er* means "performer of."
The suffix *-ful* means "full of" or "having."

Use the provided prefixes and suffixes to change each word so that it completes the sentence correctly. Then, keeping in mind that prefixes and suffixes sometimes change the part of speech, identify the part of speech of the new word by circling N for a noun, V for a verb, or ADJ for an adjective.

1. (comprehensive) Though the topic is complex, the article is written in simple language so it is _____ to readers of all levels.

    N   V   ADJ

2. (improvise) Using her skills of _____, the downed pilot created a crude shelter using parts she salvaged from the wreckage.

    N   V   ADJ

3. (tact) The students were praised for the _____ manner in which they handled the sensitive situation.   N   V   ADJ

4. (improvise) Grandfather, the _____ in the family, would rather build something using spare parts then buy it new at the store.

    N   V   ADJ

EXERCISE IV – Critical Reading

The following reading passage contains vocabulary words from this lesson.
Carefully read the passage and then choose the best answers for each of the questions that follow.

Any fruit to declare? **Restrictive** customs regulations sometimes irk international travelers, but the inconvenience is a mere **pittance** compared to the destructive potential of a single smuggled plant or animal. For evidence, one need only examine the island of Guam, the largest of
5   the Marianas Island chain in the West Pacific.

The wilderness of Guam, in its undeveloped beauty, resounded with the various calls of native birds until World War II. It was during that time, presumably, that a stealthy invader found its way from a shipping crate to the jungle, where it discovered a veritable feast—a predator's
10   paradise—of small birds, lizards, and eggs.

Unchecked by natural predators, the brown tree snake was free to indulge and procreate on Guam. By 1970, the snake could be found on every part the island, which is approximately thirty miles long by nine miles wide.

15   A warm jungle, rich with birds, lizards, and rodents, **fostered** the exploding number of brown tree snakes, each of which grows to an average of three to six feet in length. The snake, mildly poisonous, has tiny fangs in the back of its mouth that are used only if the snake has the opportunity to gnaw on its prey, so it poses little threat to adults.

20   As the reptiles prospered, the jungles grew eerily silent, save whispers of the humid Pacific breeze through the palms, or coconut crabs **scurrying** over the craggy, volcanic rocks that litter the jungle floor. By 1984, nine of Guam's twelve native bird species were extinct, as well as half the lizards, the primary food source for young snakes.

25   Brown tree snakes create more than just an ecological problem on Guam. The snakes slither up electric lines and into power boxes, causing power outages and costing time and money. They are also a source of anxiety for residents who fear that the snakes might attack their infants who cannot defend themselves.

30   Declining animal populations and frequent power problems **incited** officials to take action against the invaders, though largely to save the other islands of the Pacific. Dogs are used to sweep outgoing flights at Guam's airport and incoming flights at most destinations. Snake traps—modified minnow traps baited with mice—hang from the fences
35   surrounding airstrips. Residents are encouraged to kill any snakes they might see, though despite the infestation, the snakes are not especially easy to find. The trees on Guam are not bent, as some might believe after watching sensationalized documentaries, beneath the weight of

40 dangling snakes. As nocturnal hunters, the snakes usually curl up in dark places during the day and emerge to hunt at night. Though the snakes are thought to exceed twenty per square acre of jungle, many residents go years without spotting one—if any—in nature.

Biologists, unwilling to **cede** the jungles to the snakes, have tried for years to exterminate the invasive species, but until the perfect predator,
45 chemical, or control method is found, birds will not be abundant on the island. On the other hand, the snakes have no effect on the crystal clear waters, world-class diving, and amazing confluence of cultures on Guam, so do not allow stories about snakes to deter your travel plans. And remember, a little hassle in the airport might make you a little late, but it
50 might also prevent the destruction of an entire ecosystem.

1. As used in line 15, *fostered* most nearly means
   A. fed.
   B. supplied.
   C. provided.
   D. supported.
   E. encouraged.

2. The brown tree snakes are thought to have colonized Guam during
   A. World War I.
   B. World War II.
   C. the Korean War.
   D. 1970.
   E. 1984.

3. Which of the following is *not* listed as a part of the brown tree snake's diet?
   A. crabs.
   B. rodents.
   C. eggs.
   D. birds.
   E. lizards.

4. As used in line 30, *incited* most nearly means
   A. followed.
   B. prompted.
   C. strained.
   D. suggested.
   E. warned.

5. The author of the passage would probably agree that the brown tree
    snake problem
    A. will never be solved.
    B. has ruined the economy of Guam.
    C. has been overstated in the past.
    D. cannot spread to other islands.
    E. should be viewed as a positive experience.

Lesson Fourteen

1. **accost** (ə kôst´) *v.* to confront someone with a request or command; to approach boldly
    The mugger *accosted* the man in the alley.
    syn: detain; waylay   *ant: avoid; dodge*

2. **ascend** (ə send´) *v.* to move upward; to climb
    The mountain climber *ascended* the rock face.
    syn: rise; escalate   *ant: descend; lower*

3. **candidate** (kan´ di dāt) *n.* 1. a person running for public office
        2. a person who is considered for something, such as a prize or an honor; a prospect
    (1) The mayoral candidate posted signs throughout the city.
    (2) The company's chairman nominated three new *candidates* for the open vice-president position.
    (1) *syn: applicant; contender*
    (2) *syn: nominee*

4. **conventional** (kən ven´ shən əl) *adj.* based on accepted customs and practices
    The Navy has a few nuclear-powered vessels, but most ships in the fleet use *conventional* methods of propulsion.
    syn: common; traditional   *ant: strange; innovative*

5. **culprit** (kul´ prit) *n.* a guilty person
    Frieda vowed to catch the *culprit* who ran over her mailbox.
    syn: offender; perpetrator

6. **daft** (daft) *adj.* 1. delirious and crazy
        2. foolish
    (1) The *daft* inventor once caused an explosion that broke every window in his house.
    (2) The *daft* chef sometimes forgets to turn off the stove.
    (1) *syn: insane; batty; nutty*   *ant: rational; sensible*
    (2) *syn: dim; careless*   *ant: wise; clever*

7. **disparage** (di spar´ ij) *v.* to belittle; to denigrate
    Pauline *disparaged* anyone who did not agree with her.
    syn: detract; decry; depreciate   *ant: compliment; flatter; praise*

8. **miscellaneous** (mis ə lān′ ē əs) *adj.* consisting of different things; mixed
The junk drawer in the kitchen is full of *miscellaneous* tools and gadgets.
syn: assorted; various   *ant: uniform; identical*

9. **placard** (plak′ ärd) *n.* a sign or notice, often small
The *placards* on the sides of some trucks identify hazardous materials on board.

10. **proximity** (prok sim′ itē) *n.* closeness
The *proximity* of our house to the school allows the children to walk to class.
syn: nearness   *ant: remoteness*

11. **quarry** (kwôr′ ē) *n.* 1. the object of a chase; a hunted animal
                          2. a pit where stone is extracted from the earth
              v. to extract stone from the earth
    (n.1) After running down the wounded deer, the wild dogs feasted on their *quarry*.
    (n.2) Large dump trucks enter and leave the marble *quarry* all day long.
    (v)   Workers *quarried* the granite for the building just one mile from the work site.
    (n.1) *syn: prey; prize*   *ant: hunter*
    (v)   *syn: mine; extract*   *ant: bury*

12. **regatta** (ri gä′ tə) *n.* a boat race or series of boat races
The annual *regatta* brought thousands of spectators to the small coastal community.

13. **sordid** (sôr′ did) *adj.* immorally foul; vulgar
The police uncovered a *sordid* scheme to blackmail the senator.
syn: shameful; disgusting   *ant: pleasing; honorable*

14. **stereotype** (ster´ ē ə tīp) *n.* 1. an oversimplified image or opinion
   2. one who embodies an oversimplified image of a group
   v. to assign an oversimplified image or opinion to a group

   (n.1) A *stereotype* might suggest that everyone from Texas is a cowboy, and everyone from Maine is a fisherman.

   (n.2) Your undecorated apartment and empty refrigerator fit the *stereotype* of the bachelor lifestyle.

   (v) She incorrectly *stereotyped* the Swiss as comprising only bankers, watchmakers, and cheese makers.

   (n.1) *syn: generalization; label*

   (n.2) *syn: model; paradigm; archetype*

   (v) *syn: label; pigeonhole; categorize*

15. **whet** (wet) *v.* 1. to sharpen
   2. to stimulate or excite

   (1) They used large, smooth stones to *whet* their primitive bronze swords.

   (2) The smell of bread baking always *whets* my appetite.

   (1) *syn: hone*   *ant: dull*

   (2) *syn: rouse; encourage; trigger*   *ant: stifle; bore*

EXERCISE I – Words in Context

Using the vocabulary list for this lesson, supply the correct word to complete each sentence.

1. The cheetah had no difficulty catching its _____.

2. Police arrested the _____ immediately after the robbery.

3. The old coffee can in the garage contains _____ nuts and bolts.

4. Our _____ dog sometimes gets excited and runs into walls.

5. Fans usually _____ the famous actress for autographs when they spot her in public places.

6. The family-oriented department store refuses to sell _____ books and magazines.

7. The water was very deep, so the swimmer remained in close _____ to the shore.

8. Articles about space always _____ the curiosity of the young astronomer.

9. The teenagers disliked when adults _____ them as disrespectful troublemakers.

10. When the scuba diver runs low on air, she must _____ to the surface.

11. The crew polished the bottom of the sailboat in preparation for the _____.

12. To prevent favoritism, judges were allowed to hear, but not see, the _____ auditioning for the symphony orchestra.

13. A[n] _____ on the door read, "EMPLOYEES ONLY."

14. If you _____ the gift someone gives you, then you should not expect to receive another.

15. When _____ wisdom fails to solve a problem, you must think of new ways to solve it.

EXERCISE II – Sentence Completion

Complete the sentence in a way that shows you understand the meaning of the italicized vocabulary word.

1. After Ralph *ascended* the long stairway, he…

2. *Conventional* automobiles run on gasoline, but in the future they might…

3. The catalog lists *miscellaneous* parts and supplies for…

4. The news reporter *accosted* the woman with questions about…

5. When the wolves could find no *quarry*, they were forced to…

6. Tom *disparaged* Kristen's artwork because…

7. The restaurant *whetted* customers' appetites by…

8. Jose fits the *stereotype* of class clown because…

9. During the *regatta*, one of the speedboats…

10. The *placard* on the fuel tank warned…

11. Because of the *proximity* of the houses to the forest fire, firefighters told…

12. No one thought that the *sordid* movie should…

13. The *daft* man injured himself when he…

14. To be a *candidate* for the academic award, a student must…

15. The *culprit* disappeared in the crowd after she…

EXERCISE III – Prefixes and Suffixes

Study the entries and use them to complete the questions that follow.

The prefix *un-* means "not" or "opposite of."
The suffix *-ance* means "state of" or "quality of."
The suffix *-ion* means "act of," "state of," or "result of."
The suffix *-ist* means "doer of" or "follower of."

Use the provided prefixes and suffixes to change each word so that it completes the sentence correctly. Then, keeping in mind that prefixes and suffixes sometimes change the part of speech, identify the part of speech of the new word by circling N for a noun, V for a verb, or ADJ for an adjective.

1. (conventional)   An artist who is a[n] _____ might ignore modern trends and instead imitate the painting style of the great masters.

    N   V   ADJ

2. (ascend)   The king's _____ over the region ended with a bloody revolt.   N   V   ADJ

3. (conventional)   The engineers had to turn to _____ building methods when traditional designs failed to withstand the steady winds and frequent earthquakes.   N   V   ADJ

4. (ascend)   During the _____, the team of mountain climbers narrowly avoided an avalanche.   N   V   ADJ

EXERCISE IV – Critical Reading

The following reading passage contains vocabulary words from this lesson. Carefully read the passage and then choose the best answers for each of the questions that follow.

The next time that surprise essay test **disparages** you, or you grow weary when the clock seems to tick backwards during those last ten minutes of study hall, simply allow your blank stare to **ascend** to the ceiling, because oh, such fascinating things await you. If you are in a **conventional** classroom, you will doubtlessly
5 see the thousands of dots in the ceiling tiles and perhaps a cobweb or two, but shift your gaze instead to the light fixtures, where more than likely you will see the glowing white tubes projecting their artificial beams. What you might not see, perhaps, is the century of engineering that has gone into making those fluorescent bulbs possible. And yes, it is quite fascinating—really.
10 You do not need a degree in physics to understand how fluorescent bulbs work; a basic understanding of electricity and light will be plenty. First, electricity, simply, is the flow of electrons—the charged particles that orbit atoms. Anywhere electrons are free, current can flow. Metals such as copper or iron have many free electrons, as do charged, or ionized, gasses. Second, some atoms, such as the atoms
15 of the tungsten filament inside an ordinary light bulb, emit visible light when their electrons are excited. Other atoms emit infrared waves when they are excited, which are invisible to the naked eye but present in the form of heat energy. Next, take a look at how a fluorescent bulb works.

First, imagine, or look at, a fluorescent bulb. It is a sealed glass tube with an
20 electrode on each end. The bulb is filled with an inert gas, usually argon, and the inside of the glass is coated with phosphor powder, just like the glass on older television sets. Finally, inside the tube sits a tiny drop of mercury, the dense liquid metal found in old thermometers.

When you flip the switch for a modern fluorescent bulb, you launch a series of
25 events. First, an electric charge builds up on the electrodes until crowded electrons spring into the inert gas in the bulb, ionizing the argon atoms and thus allowing a stream of electrons, or current, to pass from one end of the bulb to the other. At the same time, the electrons vaporize the mercury and excite its atoms, too, but you see nothing because mercury emits only invisible infrared light. This is where
30 the phosphor powder comes into play. The invisible light produced by the mercury strikes the phosphor atoms and excites them. The phosphor atoms, in turn, emit the white light that gives fluorescent bulbs their heartwarming, unnatural glow.

"Great," you say, "but what's that buzzing noise?" Current passing through ionized gas has the tendency to turn into a runaway reaction as the "excitement"
35 builds in the bulb. Rather than allowing bulbs to explode, lamp-makers install a device called a *ballast* in close **proximity** to the bulbs. The ballast ensures that the current through the bulb remains steady by slowing down the chain reaction. AC current alternates rapidly, so the ballast must switch directions hundreds of times
40 each second, hence the hum.

Captivated? You do not have to be, but at least now you will have something to **whet** your curiosity when you stare at the ceiling in boredom or defeat, because counting those ceiling tiles only goes so far.

1. Which choice best explains why paragraph 1 includes the following sentence?

    And yes, it is quite fascinating—really.

    A. The sentence explains how fascinating engineering is.
    B. The author assumes that readers might disagree.
    C. The sentence is directed to readers who like science.
    D. The author is attempting to sound trendy.
    E. The sentence helps to explain fluorescent light.

2. Which choice would be the best substitute for the word *conventional* as it is used in line 4?
    A. old-fashioned
    B. modern
    C. plain
    D. clean
    E. typical

3. When electricity passes through mercury, the mercury atoms emit
    A. a light similar to that emitted by tungsten.
    B. white light.
    C. a reddish light.
    D. invisible light.
    E. inert gas.

4. As used in line 42, *whet* most nearly means
    A. halt.
    B. trigger.
    C. sharpen.
    D. fine-tune.
    E. quench.

5. The tone of the passage suggests that the author
    A. appreciates fluorescent bulbs, but dislikes them.
    B. does not approve of technology.
    C. has fluorescent lights at home.
    D. does not enjoy science, and dislikes technology.
    E. is definitely a scientist.

Lesson Fifteen

1. **arbitrary** (är´ bi trer ē) *adj.* based on preference, convenience, or chance rather than law, reason, or fact
   An appellate court overturned the judge's *arbitrary* ruling.
   syn: random; irrational   *ant: legitimate; reasoned*

2. **conspicuous** (kən spik´ yōō əs) *adj.* obvious; easy to see; attracting attention
   The *conspicuous* man was wearing a cowboy hat in the swimming pool.
   syn: noticeable; showy   *ant: disguised; ordinary*

3. **detest** (di test´) *v.* to dislike intensely; to hate
   Pam *detests* traffic, so she waits to leave work until rush hour is over.
   syn: abhor; loathe   *ant: adore; love*

4. **dexterity** (dek ster´ i tē) *n.* 1. skill in physical action
                                        2. mental quickness; cleverness
   (1) He demonstrated his superior *dexterity* by juggling four bowling pins.
   (2) The police underestimated the *dexterity* of the criminal who used a ballpoint pen to pick the locks on his shackles.
   (1) *syn: proficiency; talent*   *ant: clumsiness*
   (2) *syn: cunning; ingenuity*   *ant: incompetence*

5. **dreg** (dreg) *n.* the least desirable part (often used in plural form)
   Stray cats fought over the tasty *dregs* behind the seafood-processing factory.
   syn: lees; waste

6. **flourish** (flûr´ ish) *v.* to thrive; to prosper
                            n. a stylish ornamentation; a decoration
   (v) Not all trees *flourish* in bright, sunny conditions.
   (n) Debbie adds a beautiful *flourish* to the capital letters in her signature.
   (v) *syn: succeed; grow*   *ant: flounder; deteriorate*
   (n) *syn: enhancement; embellishment*   *ant: blemish; disfigurement*

7. **fray** (frā) *n.* a fight; a brawl
                  v. to wear away by friction
   (n) The players involved in the *fray* were ejected from the game.
   (v) The sharp rocks slowly *frayed* the mountain climber's rope.
   (n) *syn: brawl; scuffle*   *ant: peace*
   (v) *syn: unravel; tatter*

8. **incoherent** (in kō hîr´ ənt) *adj.* lacking logical connection; unclear; rambling
Roger mumbles *incoherent* phrases in his sleep.
syn: confused; disjointed　　　　　　*ant: articulate; rational*

9. **nullify** (nul´ ə fī) *v.* to make invalid; to repeal
The antidote *nullified* the effects of the deadly poison.
syn: annul; reverse　　　　　　*ant: validate; confirm*

10. **paltry** (pôl´ trē) *adj.* of little or no importance; petty
With adequate time, even a *paltry* investment now can turn into a fortune later.
syn: insignificant; trivial　　　　　　*ant: substantial; major*

11. **persistent** (pər sis´ tent) *adj.* refusing to give up; remaining for a long time
Anne's *persistent* complaining finally convinced the city to fix the pothole in front of her house.
syn: unrelenting; continual　　　　　　*ant: temporary; short*

12. **prediction** (pri dik´ shən) *n.* something foretold; a prophecy
The fan made a *prediction* that his team would win the game by eleven points.

13. **sinister** (sin´ i stər) *adj.* threatening; ominous; evil
The stone gargoyles on the building look *sinister*, but they are meant to frighten away evil spirits.
syn: menacing; frightening　　　　　　*ant: harmless; good*

14. **succinct** (sək singkt´) *adj.* clearly expressed in few words; to the point
The president delivered powerful messages in clear, *succinct* speeches.
syn: concise; pithy　　　　　　*ant: wordy; drawn-out*

15. **tundra** (tən´ drə) *n.* a treeless plain in arctic regions having permanently frozen subsoil
During the warmest summer months, the soil of the *tundra* is soft and muddy.

EXERCISE I – Words in Context

Using the vocabulary list for this lesson, supply the correct word to complete each sentence.

1. During the yard sale, Amber sold her beloved possessions for _____ sums.

2. They knew the painting was authentic because the artist's signature had a unique _____.

3. The new ruling _____ the court's previous decision.

4. The suspect was easy to find because he was driving a[n] _____ car.

5. The _____ man tried out for the team three times unsuccessfully before attempting a different sport.

6. Caribou and grizzly bears can be found walking the _____ of northern Alaska.

7. If you _____ getting animal hair on your clothes, then you should not buy a cat.

8. There was something _____ about the unmarked, black helicopters seen flying over the forest at night, far from any military base.

9. The encoded message was _____ to anyone but the spy who received it.

10. The dishonest official made a[n] _____ decision instead of actually counting the votes.

11. The _____ of society congregated beneath the abandoned highway bridge.

12. The oracle's _____ made the king uneasy.

13. Mike lost a tooth when he was punched while trying to break up the _____.

14. The teacher expressed the _____ message that cheating would result in instant failure.

15. Aldon has the natural _____ to become a world-class concert pianist.

EXERCISE II – Sentence Completion

Complete the sentence in a way that shows you understand the meaning of the italicized vocabulary word.

1. If you *detest* cold weather, then you would not want to…

2. Harriet could manage to mumble only a few *incoherent* words after…

3. The judge *nullified* the prior ruling because…

4. The lumber industry *flourished* in the small town until…

5. The lions ate the best parts of the deer and left the *dregs* to…

6. To remove the *persistent* oil stain on the driveway, Dan had to…

7. Digging into the *tundra* is difficult because…

8. No one would offer a *prediction* about…

9. Terry got into a *fray* during the concert when…

10. The young students must wear *conspicuous* T-shirts during the class field trip so the chaperones can…

11. *Succinct* communication is especially important when…

12. Everyone could tell by the *sinister* look in his eye that he…

13. Her own problems seemed *paltry* after…

14. To assure parents that none of the students' grades were *arbitrary*, the teacher showed…

15. Her superior *dexterity* allowed her to…

EXERCISE III – Prefixes and Suffixes

Study the entries and use them to complete the questions that follow.

The prefix *in-* means "in" or "not."
The suffix *-ness* means "state," "quality," or "condition."
The suffix *-ous* means "full of."
The suffix *-or* means "one who does."

Use the provided prefixes and suffixes to change each word so that it completes the sentence correctly. Then, keeping in mind that prefixes and suffixes sometimes change the part of speech, identify the part of speech of the new word by circling N for a noun, V for a verb, or ADJ for an adjective.

1. (dexterity) The many levers and buttons on the complex machine require an operator with _____ hands. N   V   ADJ

2. (conspicuous) The movie star tries to look _____ when she goes to public places.   N   V   ADJ

3. (arbitrary) Instead of taking their problems to court, the companies hired a[n] _____ to settle their dispute.
                                                          N   V   ADJ

4. (conspicuous) The _____ of the animal's markings makes it easy to identify.   N   V   ADJ

EXERCISE IV – Improving Paragraphs

Read the following passage and then answer the multiple-choice questions that follow. The questions will require you to make decisions regarding the revision of the reading selection.

1   It is difficult to ignore the **conspicuous** art style often referred to simply as *retro*. The style, characterized by long, flowing lines, rounded corners, and a streamlined general appearance, is a mainstay of classic comic books and novelty diners. It is present in the great sunbursts on the spire of the Chrysler Building and in the tapered towers of the Golden Gate Bridge. Also many forms of transportation prior to the decade of the 1950s were made in the style, such as trains, cars, and even bicycles. They look as though they are moving fast even when they are sitting still due to their design. What is this sleek style and where did it go?

2   The style widely regarded as *retro* is actually a form of *art deco,* a movement that originated in Europe in the early 1920s. There are several conflicting explanations of its exact origins, but most agree that art deco became famous at the 1925 World's Fair in Paris, where it debuted as an art form that combines fashion and function. By 1928, art deco had made it to the United States.

3   Generally, it is a marriage of the pre-industrial world and the latest in modern technology. Art deco features the rounded corners and straight lines of zeppelins, but it conveys larger-than-life themes of human ingenuity and dominance. Sculptures depict humans at their finest moments, and skyscrapers inspire the same curious wonder as the Great Sphinx or an Aztec pyramid.

4   The influence of technology increased during the 1930s, and art deco transitioned into *Streamline Moderne.* Artists began to incorporate elements of aeronautics, broadcasting, and mass-production. Sculptures, signs, and household appliances adopted the rounded corners of rocket fins and airplane wings. In 1935, Chrysler introduced its new *Air-Flow* automobile design. The public **detested** streamlined automobiles initially, but the Air-Flow design was indeed decades ahead in automotive design.

5   In its simplest form, art deco emphasizes the size, symmetry, and purpose of its subject. It imparts elegance and sophistication to the most commonplace household items, and it turns ordinary wall clocks and marble paperweights into conversation pieces even if they are not antiques. In architecture, art deco is a mighty **flourish** of man's achievement, a **prediction** of a bright future of towering skyscrapers and cities in the sky. The spire of the Empire State Building was in fact designed to be a mooring dock for blimps! Unfortunately, fleets of floating passenger-airships never quite made it past the drawing board.

6   The same factors that made it a success eventually led to its demise. As mass-production matured, art deco grew increasingly expensive. Square corners are much cheaper to manufacture than rounded, aerodynamic corners, especially for items that do not really need to be aerodynamic, like washing machines and roadside diners. The financial burden of World War II put an end to large art deco projects.

7   Though science originally inspired art deco, it eventually rendered art deco obsolete. An emerging Space Age suggested a future in space, and space is a vacuum: streamlining is of little importance beyond the atmosphere. The point was rammed home when, in 1957, a world gazed upon the Soviet Union's *Sputnik*, the first artificial satellite. It was an ugly, insect-like spheroid surrounded by antennae, and it was followed by a series of even uglier, yet functional, spacecraft.

8   Artists abandoned their dreams of sparkling chrome cities on platforms in the sky; the future would consist of cost-effective machines built for function alone. Like space, the machines would be cold and bleak—certainly nothing on which to model a dining table or lounge chair. To all but a few **persistent** collectors of art deco, the trend sailed off with the last zeppelin.

1.   Which revision shows the best way to combine the following sentences from paragraph 1?

> Also many forms of transportation prior to the decade of the 1950s were made in the style, such as trains, cars, and even bicycles. They look as though they are moving fast even when they are sitting still due to their design.

A.   Transportation looked as if it were moving when it sat still prior to the 1950s—even bicycles, trains, and cars.

B.   Art-deco also inspired transportation; prior to 1950, trains, cars, and even bicycles were designed to convey an illusion of motion and speed.

C.   The effect of motion was adhered to by cars, trains, and bicycles prior to 1950, even if these things were not moving.

D.   Art deco also inspired transportation; prior to 1950, bikes, trains, and even cars were designed to convey an illusion of motion and speed.

E.   Cars and trains prior to the 1950s looked as though they were moving even when they were sitting still; even bicycles did, because of the way they were designed.

2. The first sentence of paragraph 6 would be best improved by
   A. replacing *demise* with a better word.
   B. replacing *it* with *art deco*.
   C. adding a comma after *success*.
   D. deleting *same*.
   E. replacing *led* with *leads*.

3. Which sentence should be added to the beginning of paragraph 3?
   A. There is no **succinct** way to explain the many influences behind art deco.
   B. A series of **arbitrary** decisions eventually results in what we call art.
   C. Art deco required great **dexterity** on behalf of the artist.
   D. Space travel **nullified** the ideas behind art deco.
   E. Art deco made buildings look **sinister**, like dank, medieval castles.

4. According to the author, which choice is *neither* an influence nor theme of art deco?
   A. ancient cultures
   B. aerodynamics
   C. industry
   D. satellite technology
   E. broadcasting

Review

Lessons 13 – 15

EXERCISE I – Inferences

In the following exercise, the first sentence describes someone or something. Infer information from the first sentence, and then choose the word from the Word Bank that best completes the second sentence.

Word Bank

culprit	restrictive	incoherent	comprehensive
persistent	proximity	dexterity	miscellaneous

1. The user's manual explained how to set up the new printer, but it did not explain what to do if the printer failed to work properly.
   From this sentence, we can infer that the user's manual is not _____.

2. Holding a paddle in each hand, Samantha can beat two people at ping-pong simultaneously.
   From this sentence, we can infer that Samantha has amazing _____.

3. Over the course of a few weeks, Mark got used to the sound of the train passing in the middle of the night.
   From this sentence, we can infer that there are railroad tracks in _____ to Mark's house.

4. No arrest was made following the recent bank robbery.
   From this sentence, we can infer that the _____ is still on the loose.

5. Emily could not make any sense of the strange message scrawled on the napkin; it appeared to be some type of secret code.
   From this sentence, we can infer that the message was _____ to Emily.

EXERCISE II – Related Words

Some of the vocabulary words from lessons 13–15 have related meanings. Complete the following sentences by choosing the word that best completes the specified relationship. Some word pairs will be antonyms, some will be synonyms, and some will be words often used in the same context.

1. *Foster* is nearly opposite in meaning to the word
    A. incite.
    B. scurry.
    C. flourish.
    D. disparage.
    E. whet.

2. *Precipitate* most nearly means
    A. flounder.
    B. incite.
    C. disparage.
    D. nullify.
    E. detest.

3. The word *daft* contrasts most with the word
    A. sinister.
    B. shrewd.
    C. sordid.
    D. vigorous.
    E. incoherent.

4. If someone is *devout*, then he or she has beliefs that are
    A. miscellaneous.
    B. incoherent.
    C. persistent.
    D. arbitrary.
    E. paltry.

5. The police arrested the *culprit* and allowed the _____ to leave.
    A. candidates
    B. regatta
    C. dregs
    D. quarry
    E. bystanders

6. *Sinister* is closest in meaning to
   A. devout.
   B. shrewd.
   C. sordid.
   D. conventional.
   E. incoherent.

7. Someone who *accosts* you wants you to _____ to his or her request.
   A. cede
   B. scurry
   C. precipitate
   D. nullify
   E. detest

8. *Flourish* is most opposite in meaning to
   A. incite.
   B. spew.
   C. ascend.
   D. flounder.
   E. foster.

9. If a class is *restrictive*, then students might not acquire a[n] _____ understanding of the subject.
   A. comprehensive
   B. paltry
   C. incoherent
   D. sinister
   E. daft

10. A *succinct* second message must be sent if the first message is
    A. miscellaneous.
    B. incoherent.
    C. conspicuous.
    D. persistent.
    E. vigorous.

EXERCISE III – Crossword Puzzle

Use the clues to complete the crossword puzzle. The answers consist of vocabulary words from lessons 13 through 15.

Across

2. The child finished the milkshake and left the cup of syrupy _____ sitting on the back seat of the car.
3. The antidote will _____ the effects of the poison.
4. Ralph did not care what he read, so his library book selections were _____.
8. Every hour, the geyser _____[s] hot water into the air.
9. No one wants to sit in close _____ to Shelly because she is sick with a cold.
11. The company hired outside consultants for a new perspective when _____ thinking failed to solve the crisis.
12. The squirrels _____ up the post and steal food from the bird feeder.
13. The tiny crack in the dam was thought to be a[n] _____ concern until the water began rushing through the concrete.
14. The _____ on the truck read "FLAMMABLE."

Down

1. After a brief sprint and a flying leap, the leopard had captured its _____.
2. Playing with building blocks will help a child to develop his or her _____.
5. The company's public relations expert was chosen for her _____ in dealing with angry clients.
6. She is new to the company, but she plans to _____ the ranks quickly.
7. The speaker struck the podium with his fist and pointed at people during his _____ speech.
10. Their life savings was a mere _____ compared to the price of the new house.

Lesson Sixteen

1. **concise** (kən sīs´) *adj.* brief and to the point
   You will have only three minutes to interview the governor, so keep your questions *concise*.
   syn: short; succinct   *ant: wordy; lengthy*

2. **dubious** (dōō´ bē əs) *adj.*   1. uncertain in thought
                                        2. questionable; suspicious
   (1) Dave had a *dubious* opinion about computers until he learned how to use one.
   (2) I knew the man was impersonating a police officer when I saw his *dubious* badge.
   (1) *syn: unconvinced; undecided*   *ant: sure; confident*
   (2) *syn: suspect; fishy*   *ant: reliable; certain*

3. **dupe** (dōōp) *v.* to fool; to delude
   The crook tried to *dupe* the couple by convincing them to invest in a fictional company.
   syn: cheat; con

4. **feudal** (fyōō´ dəl) *adj.*   pertaining to the practice of sovereign lords granting land to nobles in exchange for money and military service
   In a *feudal* economic system, barons and dukes govern lands but pay taxes to the king.

5. **illegible** (il lej´ ə bəl) *adj.* incapable of being read
   The student was told to rewrite his essay because his handwriting was *illegible*.
   syn: scrawled; undecipherable   *ant: clear; neat*

6. **indigent** (in´ di jint) *adj.* poor; destitute
   The greedy king seldom considered the *indigent* peasants living beyond the castle walls.
   syn: needy; impoverished   *ant: affluent; wealthy*

7. **inhibition** (in hə bish´ ən) *n.* a mental restraint or hindrance
   Kelly's *inhibitions* prevent her from singing at the karaoke lounge.
   syn: reserve; self-consciousness   *ant: daring; bravado*

8. **merit** (mâr´ ət) *n.* 1. superior quality or worth
   2. demonstrated achievement or ability
   v. to deserve
   (n.1) Her *merits* outnumbered her faults.
   (n.2) Ursula knew that Robert had the *merit* to become a great leader.
   (v) Finding a single, Native-American arrowhead on the ground does not *merit* turning our baseball field into a full-fledged archaeological dig.
   (n.1) *syn: excellence*   *ant: incompetence*
   (n.2) *syn: capacity; capability*   *ant: inadequacy*
   (v) *syn: entitle; earn; justify*   *ant: prohibit; forbid*

9. **potent** (pōt´nt) *adj.* producing great effects; powerful
   That *potent* medicine can cause death if taken in large doses.
   syn: strong; mighty   *ant: weak; ineffective*

10. **protagonist** (prō tag´ ə nist) *n.* 1. the main character in drama or literature 2. the leader or great supporter of a cause
    (1) Throughout the course of the story, the *protagonist* grows from a young girl into an old woman.
    (2) The group's *protagonist* speaks at rallies and public gatherings.
    (1) *syn: hero/heroine; star*   *ant: antagonist*
    (2) *syn: champion*   *ant: enemy*

11. **ruse** (rōōz´) *n.* a strategic act of deception; a ploy
    The general used a *ruse* to defeat the considerably larger enemy.
    syn: stratagem; scheme

12. **straightforward** (strāt fôr´ wərd) *adj.* honest and frank; not evasive
    The politician was never known to give a simple, *straightforward* answer to a question.
    syn: candid; forthright   *ant: evasive; confusing*

13. **subsequent** (sub´ si kwent) *adj.* following in time or order; resulting
    The blizzard struck without warning, and *subsequent* snowdrifts caused the highways to close for days.
    syn: ensuing; consequent   *ant: previous; prior*

14. **vogue** (vōg) *n.* the fashion at a particular time
    People often laugh at the clothing styles that were once in *vogue*.
    syn: fad; style   *ant: anachronism*

15. **writhe** (rīth) *v.* to twist and squirm, as from pain
    Tim *writhed* in pain after breaking his ankle during the soccer match.
    syn: thrash; wriggle

EXERCISE I – Words in Context

Using the vocabulary list for this lesson, supply the correct word to complete each sentence.

1. In a[n] _____ to catch the thief, the campers pretended to be asleep.

2. Under the rules of the _____ system, barons had to provide soldiers to fight in the king's army.

3. Howard was from a wealthy family, but he wanted to achieve success on his own _____.

4. The _____ people were forced to leave town to find work.

5. The _____ announcement lasted only seconds, but it contained all the important information.

6. Reese stepped on a nail, and the _____ wound caused him to limp.

7. The _____ of the story learns a new lesson with each of her adventures.

8. Since the terrible accident, Sam has had a[n] _____ feeling about whether he wants to drive on the expressway again.

9. That music is in _____ right now, but it will be forgotten in a few months.

10. The migraine headache caused him to _____ in pain for ten minutes.

11. Pauline wanted a[n] _____ answer, but no one wanted to hurt her feelings by telling the truth.

12. No one could read the _____ message scribbled on the dusty window.

13. The _____ cleaning solution will bleach your clothes unless you dilute it with water.

14. Ursula loved the class, but she had too many _____ about speaking in public to participate in the frequent debates.

15. Sam's family _____ him by pretending that they forgot his birthday.

EXERCISE II – Sentence Completion

Complete the sentence in a way that shows you understand the meaning of the italicized vocabulary word.

1. The *protagonist* of the disaster-relief effort is often seen on television asking…

2. The salesman *duped* the customer by…

3. If the writing on the map is *illegible*, then the treasure hunters will…

4. Some clothing styles will be in *vogue* for only months, while other styles will…

5. Martin appreciates *straightforward* criticism of his music because his fans merely…

6. The company rewards employees for their *merit* by…

7. Brent's *inhibitions* prevented him from…

8. The essay you write for the test must be very *concise* because…

9. Gale tried to rid the house of the *potent* paint fumes by…

10. Jeff *writhed* in agony after he…

11. In a *ruse* to stay home from school, Liam pretended…

12. The oil tanker struck an iceberg, and the *subsequent* spill…

13. After the devastating tidal wave, many *indigent* families were…

14. In a *feudal* system, a farmer with land might be forced to…

15. The *dubious* customer entered the store just before closing time, and the clerk worried that…

EXERCISE III – Prefixes and Suffixes

Study the entries and use them to complete the questions that follow.

The prefix *de-* means "to remove" or "to reverse."
The suffix *-less* means "without" or "lacking."
The suffix *-ate* means "one who is characterized by."
The suffix *-or* means "one who does."

Use the provided prefixes and suffixes to change each word so that it completes the sentence correctly. Then, keeping in mind that prefixes and suffixes sometimes change the part of speech, identify the part of speech of the new word by circling N for a noun, V for a verb, or ADJ for an adjective.

1. (potent) The telecommunications _____ controls one of the largest corporations in the world.   N   V   ADJ

2. (merit) The student received a[n] _____ for being late to class.
          N   V   ADJ

3. (inhibition) The special paint is a rust _____, so it will help the metal last longer.   N   V   ADJ

4. (merit) Casualties were heavy, and neither side gained any ground during the _____ battle.   N   V   ADJ

EXERCISE IV – Critical Reading

The following reading passage contains vocabulary words from this lesson.
Carefully read the passage and then choose the best answers for each of the questions that follow.

Imagine living in a castle, behind heavy, protective walls of solid
stone in a building that will stand for a thousand years. Well, the **feudal**
days of kings and castles may be long gone, but that does not mean that
new castles are not available for sale or rent. There is just one minor
5   hitch: the new castles are underground.

During the 1960s, the U.S. government dug hundreds of massive
holes throughout the nation. Builders lined each hole with steel and concrete thick enough to withstand a nuclear blast. Offices, living quarters,
and recreation areas were added, and the holes became complete missile
10   silos, or parking spaces for intercontinental ballistic missiles (ICBMs),
most of which were aimed at the former Soviet Union. Doomsday did
not occur, fortunately, so, during the collapse of the Soviet Union and
the **subsequent** reduction of the U.S. nuclear stockpile, the government
disassembled the enormous missiles and abandoned the $18-million dol-
15   lar silos.

It did not take long for realtors to see the investment opportunity of
the old silos. In New York, Wyoming, California, and numerous other
states, developers purchased the silos and converted them into museums,
storage vaults, businesses, schools (one in Kansas is more than thirty
20   years old), and even homes. That's right—private underground fortress-
es! If you are **dubious** about buying one for yourself, consider that more
than twenty people have actually converted these Cold War relics into
quite livable homes.

As homes, the silos offer luxury, plenty of room (Atlas missiles stood
25   nearly 100 feet tall), security, stability, and seclusion. You will not find
this home sagging with time or needing a new roof or siding. The temperature remains a crisp 64-degrees year-round, so air conditioning is
unnecessary. One owner happily brags that tornadoes cannot harm his
underground house, and termites cannot eat it since it is lined with steel.
30   Who would not sleep soundly in a house that is safe from strong wind or
pesky insects—or wayward comets?

One Kansas family bought a silo home, as these converted facilities are
sometimes called, and added a nuclear-biological-chemical air filtration
system that will defend the silo from the most **potent** agents. Generators,
35   battery arrays, solar panels, and wind turbines ensure power will be
available during emergencies. The family even installed an underground
greenhouse and several large fish tanks in order to have a self-sustaining

food supply in addition to the stacks of canned food in the ample storage area below the living quarters. Why, you might ask? Some people col-
40 lect stamps or baseball cards. Others prepare for errant asteroids or alien invasions.

Most ordinary homes today are just over 2,000 square feet in area, but these underground mansions exceed 20,000 to 30,000 square feet, which ensures that the owner will have plenty of space for children's birthday
45 parties, guest rooms, and art collections. The silos are, of course, in **vogue** among people who enjoy privacy because it is virtually impossible to approach a silo without being seen. Thieves would **dupe** only themselves by trying to break into a silo home, unless, of course, they bring a crane that can open 100-ton blast doors.

50 There are certainly **merits** in owing a former missile silo, but these homes are definitely not for the average homebuyer; plan to spend at least a half-million dollars for a smaller, first-generation silo, and well over two million for a larger, renovated silo. They are unfurnished, but just think of the money you will save on curtains.

1. As used in line 13, the word *subsequent* most nearly means the opposite of
    A. resulting.
    B. following.
    C. subordinate.
    D. preceding.
    E. superior.

2. What is the author's intent in lines 30-31?
    A. Ridicule, because the silo-owner should know that steel eventually rusts.
    B. Humor, because it is silly to compare termite and wind damage to catastrophes of unimaginable size.
    C. Praise, because everyone wants a home that will withstand the forces of nature.
    D. Warning, because the author suggests that space is more of a threat than any nuclear war.
    E. Discredit, because no structure would be able to withstand the direct impact of a comet.

3.   The home in Kansas has all of the following *except*
     A.   a hydrogen-fuel heating system.
     B.   a wind turbine.
     C.   solar panels.
     D.   a greenhouse.
     E.   lots of storage area.

4.   As used in line 34, *potent* most nearly means
     A.   powerful and tempting.
     B.   strong and dangerous.
     C.   persuasive and intimidating.
     D.   weak and malodorous.
     E.   mild and calming.

5.   The purpose of this passage is to
     A.   compare and contrast.
     B.   persuade and advise.
     C.   inform and entertain.
     D.   appeal and convince.
     E.   ridicule and tease.

Lesson Seventeen

1. **askew** (ə skū´) *adj.* turned or twisted to one side
    The painting hung *askew*, so Marge straightened it.
    syn: crooked; slanted   *ant: straight; centered*

2. **cope** (kōp) *v.* to deal with; to endure difficulties successfully
    If you cannot change the situation, you will simply have to *cope* with it.
    syn: manage; survive   *ant: yield; surrender*

3. **deceptive** (di sep´tiv) *adj.* tending to deceive; misleading
    The *deceptive* salesman repainted retired taxi cabs and police cars and
    told buyers that they had belonged to elderly couples who seldom drove.
    syn: dishonest; shifty   *ant: truthful; genuine*

4. **engrossed** (en grōsd´) *adj.* deeply involved; absorbed
    He was so *engrossed* in the book that he did not notice that the door was
    opening slowly.
    syn: engaged; immersed   *ant: distracted; inattentive*

5. **facilitate** (fə sil´i tāt) *v.* to make easier
    To *facilitate* the renovations, we moved most of the furniture out of the
    house and into the garage.
    syn: help; aid   *ant: obstruct; hinder*

6. **gusto** (gus´tō) *n.* enthusiastic enjoyment; delight
    The food critic loves her job and performs her duties with *gusto*.
    syn: enthusiasm; zest   *ant: boredom; indifference*

7. **premise** (prem´is) *n.* an idea or statement upon which an argument is
    based or from which a conclusion is drawn; a belief
    Before going to prison, Lloyd had stolen money from the cash register on
    the *premise* that his employer did not pay him enough.

8. **rejuvenate** (ri jōō´və nāt) *v.* to restore youth; to restore to new or
    original condition
    The makers of the new lotion claim that it will *rejuvenate* skin by remov-
    ing wrinkles.
    syn: renew; revitalize   *ant: exhaust; wear*

9. **remote** (rē mōt´) *adj.* distant; far away
    The *remote* village in the mountains receives few visitors.
    syn: secluded; isolated   *ant: nearby; close*

10. **reprehensible** (rep ri hen´ sə bəl) *adj.* deserving reprimand; blameworthy
    He did not try to make excuses for his *reprehensible* crime.
    syn: guilty; awful   *ant: praiseworthy; innocent*

11. **reverberate** (ri vûr´ bə rāt) *v.* to echo repeatedly
    Cheers from spectators *reverberated* throughout the stadium.
    syn: resound; ring

12. **speculate** (spek´ ū lāt) *v.* 1. to consider a topic; to contemplate
                                        2. to purchase with the expectation of making a profit
    (1) Everyone *speculated* about what would happen in the sequel to the popular movie.
    (2) Diamond Joe *speculates* by buying up vacant lots for minimal prices.
    (1) *syn: suppose; wonder*
    (2) *syn: gamble; venture*

13. **supplement** (sup´ lə ment) *n.* something added to complete or strengthen the whole
                                    v. to add something to
    (n) The elderly woman takes *supplements* that contain extra vitamins for her joints.
    (v) The power lifter *supplements* his diet with extra protein.
    (n) *syn: addition; enhancement*
    (v) *syn: improve; enhance; complement*   *ant: reduce; diminish*

14. **vain** (vān) *adj.* 1. not having the desired effect; fruitless
                            2. excessively proud of oneself; conceited
    (1) The squirrel tried in *vain* to escape from the empty barrel, but it could not climb the shiny metal walls.
    (2) The *vain* woman secretly scorned anyone who did not complement her gown.
    (1) *syn: futile; ineffective*   *ant: successful; productive*
    (2) *syn: arrogant; proud*   *ant: humble; modest*

15. **yen** (yen) *n.* a strong desire
    Marge has a *yen* for travel, but she seldom has the time.
    syn: longing; yearning   *ant: objection; rejection*

EXERCISE I – Words in Context

Using the vocabulary list for this lesson, supply the correct word to complete each sentence.

1. Counselors will help the families of crash victims _____ with their loss.

2. The fertilizer pellets _____ the withered plant, making it green again.

3. The sound of the single shot _____ across the hilly countryside.

4. Kim kept her sprained foot raised to _____ the healing process.

5. Shelley will proceed with the plan on the _____ that Phil and Jonas will bring the supplies.

6. Mandy's _____ remark got her grounded for three days.

7. Her _____ for success was to become famous, but how, she did not know.

8. The police refused to _____ about who was guilty until they had collected more evidence.

9. Confident that her studies would pay off, Haley took the exam with _____.

10. After the earthquake, the small building sat _____.

11. The _____ man cannot walk past a mirror without looking into it.

12. Some people _____ their diets with vitamins.

13. The government chose a[n] _____ location in the Pacific Ocean to test the new missile.

14. The fine print beneath the _____ advertisement explained that the sale prices were not guaranteed.

15. The scientist locked herself in the lab so she could become _____ in her work.

EXERCISE II – Sentence Completion

Complete the sentence in a way that shows you understand the meaning of the italicized vocabulary word.

1. With *gusto*, the kindergartners proudly…

2. The *premise* of the latest movie is that it is wrong for people to…

3. A shriek *reverberated* through the halls shortly after…

4. Dad's necktie is always *askew* because he…

5. In *vain*, the lost hiker tried…

6. Translators were brought in to *facilitate*…

7. The pirate captain found a *remote* island where…

8. He always had a *yen* to travel, so he…

9. Patrick's *reprehensible* behavior did not stop until…

10. You can help them *cope* with the loss by…

11. Race fans *speculated* about…

12. Jack *supplements* his income by…

13. Weary from working the late shift for a month, Kim decided to *rejuvenate* herself by going…

14. The *deceptive* spy had little trouble persuading the guard to…

15. When the doctor is *engrossed* in his work, it is difficult for anyone to…

EXERCISE III – Prefixes and Suffixes

Study the entries and use them to complete the questions that follow.

The suffix -*ary* means "related to."
The suffix -*ion* means "act of," "state of," or "result of."
The suffix -*ive* means "tending to."
The suffix -*or* means "one who does."

Use the provided prefixes and suffixes to change each word so that it completes the sentence correctly. Then, keeping in mind that prefixes and suffixes sometimes change the part of speech, identify the part of speech of the new word by circling N for a noun, V for a verb, or ADJ for an adjective.

1. (facilitate) During the meeting, the _____ ensured that no one spoke beyond his or her time limit.   N   V   ADJ

2. (facilitate)   The returns desk at the department store made some _____ changes to handle larger numbers of customers.
   N   V   ADJ

3. (deceptive) The elaborate _____ was meant to trick the special agent into believing that he was in another country when he woke up.
   N   V   ADJ

4. (supplement) The medicine included a sheet of _____ information about the chemicals in the pills.   N   V   ADJ

EXERCISE IV – Critical Reading

The following reading passage contains vocabulary words from this lesson. Carefully read the passage and then choose the best answers for each of the questions that follow.

(1) After humans, chimpanzees and gorillas are among the smartest animals on earth, and even dolphins show an ability to classify objects by size, shape, and color. (2) Soon, another creature may be joining the small group of famously smart animals: the corvid.

(3) Crows and ravens are the most recognizable members of the family *corvidae*. (4) Jays and magpies are also a part of the group. (5) Because corvids have the ability to **cope** with changing habitats, they can be found on every continent except Antarctica.

(6) Even as expanding human populations take over the wilderness and threaten more vulnerable species, corvids are figuring out ways to use people to their own advantage. (7) Ravens and crows gather around garbage dumps and parking lots and **supplement** their diets with food that requires no hunting or exposure to dangerous predators. (8) The speed with which they adapt is a clear sign that they learn quickly.

(9) Corvids also have abilities scientists once **speculated** to be characteristic of humans alone. (10) The birds can identify numerous objects from memory, and, amazingly, they can use tools. (11) Crows, for instance, have been observed using hooked branches to **facilitate** the removal of food from tree cavities; strong evidence suggests that crows actually know how to fashion the simple tools. (12) They can also remember the hiding places for thousands of seeds, even when the seeds are hidden in **remote** locations or buried under several feet of snow.

(13) It does not stop at creativity and memory. (14) Certain members of the corvid family have the ability to mimic and learn human speech. (15) Ravens seem to have a **yen** for it; they can acquire large, complex vocabularies. (16) The phenomenon has become common knowledge thanks to literature such as Edgar Allen Poe's poem, "The Raven," in which a grieving man is driven to madness by a raven that croaks, "Nevermore!"

(17) Because of their dark color and obvious intelligence, ravens and crows have long been included in mythology and folklore around the world. (18) In Inuit and Eskimo legends, Raven is the creator of the world. (19) In Norse mythology, thought and memory materialize as ravens sitting on the shoulders of Thor; each day the birds circle the world and then report their news to Thor in the evening. (20) Corvids are symbols of death in some cultures, and divine messengers in others. (21) Some cultures simply regard crows as pests that scavenge trash and spread disease; however, the fact that crows are smart enough to identify a plastic bag as a source of food is testament to their capacity.

1. The author mentions primates and dolphins in sentence 1 to
    A. introduce the topic of clever animals.
    B. contrast them with crows and ravens.
    C. provide examples of animals affected by changing habitats.
    D. show that they too are types of *corvidae*.
    E. explain the purpose of smart animals.

2. The best substitute for the word *facilitate* in sentence 11 would be
    A. simplify.
    B. prevent.
    C. speed up.
    D. ease.
    E. suggest.

3. According to the passage, it is not certain whether corvids have the ability to
    A. learn human speech.
    B. make tools.
    C. identify manmade food sources.
    D. adapt quickly.
    E. remember.

4. As used in sentence 15, *yen* most nearly means
    A. devotion.
    B. aversion.
    C. desire.
    D. interest.
    E. fascination.

5. Which choice would be the most appropriate title for this passage?
    A. The World's Most Intelligent Animals
    B. How Crows Compare
    C. Threatened Animals
    D. The Clever Corvid
    E. Primates, Dolphins, and Crows

Lesson Eighteen

1. **asset** (as´ et) *n.* a useful or valuable person or thing
    No one was sure about the new player, but he proved to be an *asset* to the team.
    syn: benefit; boon   *ant: disadvantage; handicap*

2. **construe** (kən strōō´) *v.* to interpret the meaning of; to explain
    The ambassador from Earth offered his hand, and the aliens *construed* the gesture as an act of peace.
    syn: decipher   *ant: confuse; muddle*

3. **equilibrium** (ēk wə lib´ rē əm) *n.* a state of balance; stability
    The dehydrated messenger desperately needed water to restore his *equilibrium*.
    syn: steadiness; evenness   *ant: imbalance*

4. **imperturbable** (im pər tûr´ bə bəl) *adj.* not easily excited or upset
    The *imperturbable* man has worked on a bomb squad for eleven years.
    syn: composed; collected   *ant: excitable; edgy*

5. **interloper** (in´ tər lō pər) *n.* 1. one who meddles in the business of others
    2. an intruder
    (1) The *interloper* tried to stop the parade by lying down in the middle of the street.
    (2) Ushers escorted the *interloper* to the exit when he failed to produce a ticket.
    (1) *syn: meddler; nuisance*   *ant: helper; collaborator*
    (2) *syn: trespasser; invader*

6. **melancholy** (mel´ ən kol ē) *n.* sadness; gloom
    adj. sad; depressed
    Melancholy shrouded the party when the family heard the bad news.
    (n) *syn: depression; misery*   *ant: happiness; glee*
    (adj) *syn: dismal; somber*   *ant: optimistic; joyful*

7. **petty** (pet´ ē) *adj.* of small importance; trivial
    The detective explained to the rookie that there is no such thing as a *petty* clue.
    syn: minor; insignificant   *ant: major; essential*

8. **potential** (pə ten´ shəl)   *n.*   ability not yet used or developed
   adj.   capable of being or happening
   (n)   The student had the *potential* to become a great leader.
   (adj)   Zoo patrons must not forget the *potential* hazards of standing too close to animal cages.
   (n)   *syn: aptitude; capability*   *ant: weakness; disability*
   (adj)   *syn: possible; likely*   *ant: improbable; doubtful*

9. **prudent** (prōōd´ nt)   *adj.*   cautious and sensible
   The most *prudent* route across the mountains proved to be easier than the others.
   syn: discreet; shrewd   *ant: irresponsible; reckless*

10. **suave** (swäv)   *adj.*   having refined charm; pleasant in manner
    Laura asked her two rowdy sons to be *suave* little gentlemen during the wedding ceremony.
    syn: polished; debonair   *ant: rude; vulgar*

11. **tertiary** (tur´ shē er ē)   *adj.*   third in order, place, or importance
    The assistant to the vice president has *tertiary* authority within the company.

12. **unabated** (un ə bā´ tid)   *adj.*   continuing at full intensity
    The plague spread *unabated* until vaccines could be distributed.
    syn: unrelenting; persistent   *ant: diminishing; dwindling*

13. **unique** (ū nēk´)   *adj.*   without equal; one of a kind
    The antique rocking chair is *unique* because it was made only for Patrick Henry.
    syn: sole; unmatched   *ant: common; ordinary*

14. **vie** (vī)   *v.*   to strive for superiority or victory
    The rivals at the office both *vied* for the open manager position, but the company hired a new person for the job.
    syn: compete; contend   *ant: yield; succumb*

15. **wither** (with´ ər)   *v.*   to dry up; to shrivel
    The young plants *withered* without water.
    syn: wilt; desicate   *ant: flourish; bloom*

EXERCISE I – Words in Context

Using the vocabulary list for this lesson, supply the correct word to complete each sentence.

1. The _____ hound dog never snapped at the kittens, even as they nipped at his ears and clawed at his tail.

2. Miles wanted to purchase a[n] _____ gift for Rena, not simply something he could buy at the mall.

3. Bobby _____ his mother's smile as permission to keep the stray dog.

4. The floral bouquet _____ after sitting on the heater for a few hours.

5. The tent's primary purpose is to create shade, its secondary purpose is to keep us dry, and its _____ purpose is to provide a place to store the food and refreshments.

6. The _____ writer expressed her despair with poetry.

7. Winona's _____ fiancé quickly earned the respect of her family during dinner.

8. When the company went bankrupt, it was forced to sell all its _____.

9. Security guards escorted the _____ from the private party.

10. Police would rather solve murders than enforce laws prohibiting _____ crimes such as littering or jaywalking.

11. During the race, two hundred contestants _____ for the first-place trophy.

12. The _____ investor seldom took risks with his money.

13. The man walking the tightrope re-established his _____ before taking another step.

14. A grapefruit-sized chunk of uranium has the _____ to power an entire city for a day.

15. Two hours of _____ thunder and lightning kept everyone awake.

EXERCISE II – Sentence Completion

Complete the sentence in a way that shows you understand the meaning of the italicized vocabulary word.

1. During the television commercial, a *suave* voice describes...

2. An *interloper* hiding beneath the table heard...

3. Cory is *prudent* with his allowance, but his brother likes to...

4. Her criticism continued *unabated* until her friend told her...

5. With her talent, Mina has the *potential* to...

6. The *imperturbable* guard does not allow troublemakers to...

7. Stan refused to argue about something as *petty* as...

8. The lettuce *withered* because...

9. Though he could not read, Penn *construed* the skull and crossbones on the sign as...

10. Vendors at the carnival *vied* for customers by...

11. Winona was *melancholy* for weeks after...

12. The antique bracelet is *unique* because...

13. The *equilibrium* of the lake was disturbed when...

14. After seeing two specialists about his ailment, Dominic decided to get a *tertiary* opinion from...

15. Renee is an *asset* to the company because she...

EXERCISE III – Prefixes and Suffixes

Study the entries and use them to complete the questions that follow.

The prefix *im-* means "not" or "without."
The suffix *-ence* means "state of" or "quality of."
The suffix *-ity* means "state of" or "quality of."
The suffix *-ly* means "like."

Use the provided prefixes and suffixes to change each word so that it completes the sentence correctly. Then, keeping in mind that prefixes and suffixes sometimes change the part of speech, identify the part of speech of the new word by circling N for a noun, V for a verb, or ADJ for an adjective.

1. (imperturbable) It takes months for prison guards to develop the _____ necessary for enduring daily harassment from the inmates.

   N   V   ADJ

2. (prudent) Owing to her _____ shopping spree at the mall, Rosa did not have enough money to pay her electric bill.

   N   V   ADJ

3. (potential) The sun's rays are _____ hazardous to people who burn easily.

   N   V   ADJ

4. (prudent) With great _____, the pharmacist measured out the potent medication and bottled it for the customer.

   N   V   ADJ

EXERCISE IV – Improving Paragraphs

Read the following passage and then answer the multiple-choice questions that follow. The questions will require you to make decisions regarding the revision of the reading selection.

(1) Some scientists suggest that a planet having conditions favorable to human life, if indeed there is another one out there, would have the most **potential** for alien life; however, the discovery of *extremophiles* has forced them to reconsider. (2) No, extremophiles are not young adults who leap from helicopters and snowboard down the sides of active volcanoes while guzzling caffeinated soda; they are **unique** microorganisms that can withstand environmental conditions so extreme that they seem to defy the basic facts we know about sustaining life.

(3) Hundreds of extremophile species have been discovered, and they are usually classified by the specific environments in which they thrive and gaining membership into the various groups is no **petty** task. (4) *Thermophiles* prosper in temperatures exceeding 140° F (water boils at 212° F). (5) *Halophiles* maintains their **equilibrium** in places salty enough to cause most bacteria to **wither** and die. (6) *Acidophiles* flourish in environments having a pH of less than 3.0—roughly the acidity of lemon juice or vinegar.

(7) The first extremophiles shown were thermophiles. (8) In the 1960s, scientists found the organisms living in the hot springs of Yellowstone National Park in Wyoming, where geothermal vents heat the ground water. (9) In recent years, even tougher organisms have been found living near hydrothermal vents on the ocean floor. (10) These new bacteria-like microbes are called *hyperthermophiles* because they thrive **unabated** in 250° temperatures (possible only because the high pressure at the ocean floor raises the boiling point of the water).

(11) The heat-loving germs have cousins on the opposite end of the thermometer. (12) *Psychrophiles* live their long lives suspended in chunks of ice in frozen Antarctic lakes. (13) These cold creatures are most comfortable at –60° F or below, and they are thought to be at least 400,000 years old.

(14) *Endoliths* would be the first life forms to rave about the nutritional value of minerals; after all, these creatures eat nothing but iron, potassium, or sulfur. (15) Living inside rocks and hardened lava flows miles beneath the surface of the earth, endoliths breath hydrogen and reproduce approximately once every 100 years.

(16) Most impressive, perhaps, is the extremophile *deinococcus radiodurans*, or "Conan the Bacterium," to its friends. (17) A fatal dose of radiation to a human would not even give this mighty germ a sunburn; in fact, it takes 3,000 times the lethal dose to broil this bacteria thanks to its self-repairing genes. (18) This fearsome germ also has natural protection against pressure and tempera-

ture extremes as well a **tertiary** immunity to toxic chemicals. (19) It is truly the germ that hangs out in places where other germs do not—places like nuclear reactors.

(20) Extremophiles are as useful as they are amazing. (21) With some minor gene modification, germs with extreme tastes can be modified to eat toxic chemicals and pollutants. (22) Other extremophiles have been altered to produce antibiotics, and the way in which extremophiles **vie** for survival might someday show researchers a better way to fight diseases such as cancer. (23) Some bacteria are so large that they are visible to the naked eye! (24) Finally, extremophiles prove that life can thrive in other-than-ideal conditions, which opens a realm of possibility for those hoping to find traces of life on harsh planets. (25) Such a discovery might not be as immediately important as cleaning up the environment or curing cancer, but it will certainly give us something to anticipate.

1. Which choice shows the best way to revise the underlined portion of sentence 3 as shown below?

    > Hundreds of extremophile species have been discovered, and they are usually classified by the specific environments <u>in which they thrive and gaining membership</u> into the various groups is no **petty** task.

    A. in which they thrive. Gaining membership
    B. in which they thrive, because gaining membership
    C. in which they thrive, but gaining membership
    D. in which they thrive; and gaining membership
    E. in which they thrive: gaining membership

2. The best revision for sentence 7 would be which of the following?
    A. No one knew about extremophiles until thermophiles were discovered in the 1960s.
    B. The last extremophiles to be discovered were thermophiles.
    C. The first thermophiles were discovered to be extremophiles.
    D. Thermophiles were the first extremophiles discovered.
    E. Thermophiles are the most widespread species of extremophiles.

3. Which sentence should be deleted from the final paragraph?
    A. sentence 21
    B. sentence 22
    C. sentence 23
    D. sentence 24
    E. sentence 25

4. The introductory sentence of the passage suggests that
    A. extremophiles could exist on a planet that is not similar to Earth.
    B. the closer a planet resembles Earth, the greater the chance is that extremophiles will be found there.
    C. extremophiles cannot exist in conditions that are not favorable to humans.
    D. humans would probably not be found on a planet inhabited by extremophiles.
    E. extremophiles exist on Earth, but will probably not be found on another Earth-like planet.

Review

Lessons 16 – 18

EXERCISE I – Inferences

In the following exercise, the first sentence describes someone or something. Infer information from the first sentence, and then choose the word from the Word Bank that best completes the second sentence.

Word Bank

dubious	interloper	illegible	engrossed
prudent	potent	imperturbable	remote

1. Kyle did not realize the low water level of the river until after he had jumped off the old railroad bridge.
    From this sentence, we can infer that Kyle's decision to jump was not
    _____.

2. The village is deep in the mountains, hundreds of miles from the nearest developed city.
    From this sentence, we can infer that the location of the village is
    _____.

3. The corporation fired the new employee when it learned that he was simply an undercover reporter.
    From this sentence, we can infer that the reporter was a[n] _____.

4. A single drop of the solution is enough to kill all the weeds on the front lawn.
    From this sentence, we can infer that the solution is _____.

5. The teacher returned Ted's handwritten essay and told him to rewrite it so that it was readable.
    From this sentence, we can infer that Ted's original essay was _____.

EXERCISE II – Related Words

Some of the vocabulary words from lessons 16–18 have related meanings. Complete the following sentences by choosing the word that best completes the specified relationship. Some word pairs will be antonyms, some will be synonyms, and some will be words often used in the same context.

1. A *straightforward* answer should not be expected from someone who is
   A. melancholy.
   B. unique.
   C. deceptive.
   D. subsequent.
   E. indigent.

2. The word most similar to *speculate* is
   A. vie.
   B. writhe.
   C. dupe.
   D. construe.
   E. facilitate.

3. *Potent* is opposite in meaning to
   A. petty.
   B. prudent.
   C. straightforward.
   D. tertiary.
   E. imperturbable.

4. He had a *yen* for fame, but his _____ prevented him from doing anything that might draw attention.
   A. ruses
   B. assets
   C. inhibitions
   D. interlopers
   E. premises

5. If the new plant does not *vie* for nourishment with others, it will _____ and die.
   A. supplement
   B. writhe
   C. construe
   D. rejuvenate
   E. wither

6. A person does not earn a *reprehensible* reputation by living a[n]
   _____ lifestyle.
   A. dubious
   B. prudent
   C. vain
   D. deceptive
   E. askew

7. Someone who appears to be *imperturbable* might simply be _____
   in thought.
   A. suave
   B. unabated
   C. engrossed
   D. straightforward
   E. feudal

8. He appreciated her *concise* comment after receiving hours of _____
   criticism.
   A. unabated
   B. unique
   C. melancholy
   D. indigent
   E. subsequent

9. The *melancholy* teammate is not likely to have the _____ to play in
   today's game.
   A. gusto
   B. asset
   C. premise
   D. vogue
   E. equilibrium

10. The *interloper* might try to ruin the plans of the
   A. inhibition.
   B. potential.
   C. ruse.
   D. merit.
   E. protagonist.

EXERCISE III – Crossword Puzzle

Use the clues to complete the crossword puzzle. The answers consist of vocabulary words from lessons 16 through 18.

Across

3. Ian _____[s] his income by delivering pizzas at night.
5. The sign on the door hung _____, so Tom straightened it.
6. Frequent communication will _____ the complex job.
7. Johnny _____[d] in the dentist chair when he saw the dentist holding a large syringe.
9. After locking the deadbolt and setting the alarm, Rachel leaned a chair against the door as a[n] _____ security measure.
11. Craig was _____ about the assignment because he had missed class for the last two days.
13. The firefighter braved a[n] _____ roof collapse to save the child from the burning building.
14. The sign advertising a sale was merely a[n] _____ to lure people into the store.
15. A truck carrying tomatoes overturned on the highway, and the _____ mess took two days to clean up.

Down

1. The _____ residents are lucky to earn more than a few dollars a month.
2. The ship cannot sail until the raging seas return to a state of _____.
4. The book is based on the _____ that the lost city of Atlantis sits beneath the Mediterranean Sea.
8. The mad scientist conducts secret experiments in his _____ castle, deep in the mountains.
10. The _____ gentleman spoke like a polite scholar and never failed to smile.
12. The painting is _____ because it is the only portrait known to have been painted by the artist.

Lesson Nineteen

1. **adverse** (ad vûrs´) *adj.* acting against; harmful or unfavorable
The patient's *adverse* reaction to the medicine was nearly fatal.
syn: antagonistic; detrimental   *ant: positive; favorable*

2. **alliance** (ə lī´ əns) *n.* a union or association of groups based on
common interest
Several nations formed an *alliance* in order to defeat the invading troops.
syn: partnership; collaboration   *ant: hostility; conflict*

3. **altruism** (al´ trōō iz əm) *n.* unselfish concern for the well being of others
If not for the *altruism* of sponsors, the children's shelter would not exist.
syn: selflessness; unselfishness   *ant: egoism; selfishness; self-interest*

4. **blunder** (blun´ dûr) *n.* a serious mistake caused by ignorance or
carelessness *v.* to make a serious mistake
   (n) The mechanic's *blunder* during the repair job caused irreversible
   damage to the engine.
   (v) Jack *blundered* the haircut when he accidentally cut off too much of
   the customer's hair.
   (n) *syn: error; oversight*   *ant: triumph; accomplishment*
   (v) *syn: foul; goof*

5. **bolster** (bōl´ stər) *v.* to support and strengthen
Hundreds of signatures *bolstered* the neighborhood's effort to stop construction of the new development.
syn: aid; reinforce   *ant: hinder; obstruct*

6. **brazen** (brā´ zən) *adj.* rudely bold; shameless
The actress snubbed her fans in a *brazen* act of arrogance.
syn: insolent; defiant   *ant: decent; upright*

7. **indifferent** (in dif´ rənt, in dif´ ər ənt) *adj.* having no concern or interest
Sam was *indifferent* about what to eat for dinner, so he asked Tina to decide.
syn: impartial; nonchalant   *ant: enthusiastic; biased*

8. **insurgent** (in sûr´ jənt) *adj.* revolting against authority, especially the
government *n.* one who revolts
   (adj) Members of the *insurgent* group believed that they had no obligation
   to pay taxes.
   (n) The *insurgents* held hostages in the building and fired at troops from
   the rooftop.
   (adj) *syn: rebellious*   *ant: loyal; obedient*
   (n) *syn: rebel*   *ant: loyalist*

9. **lucid** (lōō´ sid) *adj.* easily understood; rational and clear
The geologist gave the people a *lucid* explanation of continental drift.
syn: comprehensible; obvious   *ant: confusing; muddled*

10. **mutual** (myōō´ chōō əl) *adj.* 1. directed by each toward the other; reciprocal
2. common to each party involved
(1) The two old rivals still shared a *mutual* dislike for each other.
(2) The couple first met during a party at the home of a *mutual* friend.
(1) *syn: reciprocal; shared*   *ant: private; separate*
(2) *syn: common; joint*

11. **quaint** (kwānt) *adj.* pleasingly odd or unusual; charmingly different
Grandmother sold her house and moved into a *quaint* cottage next to the shore.
syn: curious   *ant: typical; normal*

12. **retort** (ri tôrt´) *v.* to reply, especially with a quick, witty, or harsh response
n. a quick, witty reply or counterargument
(v) John *retorted* before Cindy had a chance to turn around and walk away.
(n) The stand-up comedian had a hilarious *retort* for every heckler.

13. **technology** (tek näl´ ə jē) *n.* the application of scientific knowledge to commerce, industry, or other practical purposes
Advances in *technology* make it possible to build computers smaller and faster than ever before.

14. **terminal** (tûr´ mə nəl) *adj.* 1. pertaining to or occurring at the end, limit, or extremity
2. causing or approaching death
(1) With limbs outstretched, a falling human will have a *terminal* velocity of about 125 miles per hour.
(2) Murdock's attempt to hike through the blizzard was a *terminal* mistake.
(1) *syn: final*   *ant: beginning; initial*
(2) *syn: fatal; lethal*   *ant: harmless; safe; benign*

15. **vigil** (vij´ əl) *n.* 1. a watch kept during sleeping hours
2. an observance conducted on the eve of a religious festival
(1) The town held a *vigil* in observance of the missing child.
(2) The *vigil* takes place on the evening before the most important day of the church calendar.

EXERCISE I – Words in Context

Using the vocabulary list for this lesson, supply the correct word to complete each sentence.

1. The community held a candlelight _____ to honor the fallen hero.

2. The spy infiltrated the _____ group responsible for the uprising.

3. The average human lifespan increases with each advance in medical _____.

4. Kate and Charlie expressed their _____ concern for their son's education.

5. The charity worker's large salary convinced some people that _____ was not his real motivation.

6. A good pilot must be able to stay calm and make good decisions during the most _____ conditions.

7. The company _____ security in the warehouse by installing alarms and security cameras.

8. It would soon be obvious to everyone that Ted had _____ when he added salt instead of sugar to the cookie dough.

9. People in the village sought a[n] _____ explanation for the mysterious lights they saw over the forest last night.

10. In a[n] _____ act of defiance, Dale tore up the parking ticket and let the pieces fall to the officer's feet.

11. She converted the _____, Victorian estate into a popular bed-and-breakfast.

12. Adam is usually very quiet, so Jen was surprised to hear his _____ to her joke about him.

13. A[n] _____ between the settlers and the natives ensured a temporary peace.

14. The _____ entry on the captain's log offered no explanation for the mysterious disappearance of the crew.

15. As long as no one damages the flowers, Denise is _____ about neighbor children playing on her front lawn.

EXERCISE II – Sentence Completion

Complete the sentence in a way that shows you understand the meaning of the italicized vocabulary word.

1. During the *vigil*, friends of the deceased remembered his...

2. Amy tried to form a *lucid* picture in her head of what she wanted to paint before she even...

3. The corporate spy steals *technology* from one company and then...

4. The two neighbors must reach a *mutual* agreement about the location of the property line before they can...

5. Melanie was proud of her *quaint* collection of garden gnomes, but the neighbors thought...

6. The airplane cannot make its *terminal* approach until...

7. The boss is *indifferent* about how we do the work as long as...

8. The soldiers used large rocks and timbers to *bolster*...

9. We will have to wait for the *adverse* weather to pass before we can...

10. Everyone knew that Lenny's work was pure *altruism* because he...

11. Her *brazen* attitude did not help...

12. Eric angrily *retorted* when...

13. The ambassador told her staff that one *blunder* during the peace talks could...

14. The *alliance* between the two manufacturers created...

15. The *insurgent* was imprisoned after soldiers caught him trying...

EXERCISE III – Prefixes and Suffixes

Study the entries and use them to complete the questions that follow.

The prefix *mis-* means "wrongly."
The prefix *re-* means "back" or "again."
The suffix *-ary* means "related to."
The suffix *-ate* means "to become" or "to cause to become."

Use the provided prefixes and suffixes to change each word so that it completes the sentence correctly. Then, keeping in mind that prefixes and suffixes sometimes change the part of speech, identify the part of speech of the new word by circling N for a noun, V for a verb, or ADJ for an adjective.

1. (alliance) The tumultuous marriage first appeared to be a[n] _____ of two equally stubborn people, but the couple grew beyond their differences and stayed together for the next forty years.

    N   V   ADJ

2. (terminal) The Internet service provider will _____ your service if you forget to pay the monthly fee.   N   V   ADJ

3. (alliance) Though the two nations had not fought together for decades, a[n] _____ would be necessary for them to defeat their common enemy.   N   V   ADJ

4. (adverse) At every opportunity, Dora's _____ opposed her advancement at the company.   N   V   ADJ

EXERCISE IV – Critical Reading

The following reading passage contains vocabulary words from this lesson. Carefully read the passage and then choose the best answers for each of the questions that follow.

Pirates have inspired countless tales of adventure and romance on the high seas, but to a budding nation, pirates are anything but romantic. For more than five centuries, the Barbary States on the North African coast consisted of pirate-towns—tiny kingdoms ruled by *pashas*, or military
5   leaders, and funded by the **brazen** theft of goods from merchant vessels on the Mediterranean Sea. Morocco, Algiers, Tunis, and Tripoli were homes to thugs, raiders, and looters who seized ships, plundered their goods, and then ransomed the crews or sold them into slavery.

England and France occasionally battled the pirates but ultimately
10   paid heavy tribute to guarantee the safe passage of ships—a deal having few **mutual** benefits. Each payment of "protection" money **bolstered** the pirate fleet, increased trade expenses, and set the price for hijackings yet to come.

Before the American Revolution, U.S. vessels enjoyed the protection
15   of the British Navy, and an **alliance** with France ensured their protection during the war; however, in 1783, well before the United States could build a substantial navy, the protection ceased. Pirates captured two ships in 1785 and demanded $60,000 ransom, which the U.S. eventually paid. Thomas Jefferson condemned the decision to pay; he thought it would
20   be a **blunder** to surrender to the criminals' demands because it would simply encourage more piracy. He was right. By 1800, tribute and ransom to the Barbary pirates accounted for approximately twenty percent of the national budget.

Increasing demands for tribute outraged the American public. When
25   the pasha of Tripoli demanded a gift of $225,000 from newly elected President Jefferson in 1801, the United States **retorted** with a squadron of warships. Tripoli declared war on American shipping, and for two years, U.S. ships battled pirates and attempted to blockade the Tripoli harbor. In 1803, pirates captured the *U.S.S. Philadelphia* and her crew. In a dar-
30   ing operation, American sailors disguised as pirates sailed into the Tripoli harbor and set the *Philadelphia* ablaze to deny her use by the pirates. U.S. warships shelled Tripoli months later, but made no progress until 1805, when American Marines, Arab horsemen, and Turkish and Greek mercenaries seized control of the Tripoli port town of Derna. The attack
35   drove the pasha to establish a treaty with the United States, and the battle is now commemorated in the line of the Marines' Hymn, "…to the shores of Tripoli."

The events now known as the First Barbary War established credibility for the young United States as a world power, but the war was not the
40   **terminal** blow to piracy in the Mediterranean. Distracted by the War of 1812, the United States was forced to pay ransom when Algerian pirates captured U.S. ships and held the crews hostage; however, immediately after the war, the United States sent ten ships to attack Algiers. In an interesting reversal, the U.S. Navy captured several pirate ships and ransomed
45   the crew to Algiers. In 1815, at the end of the Second Barbary War, Algiers submitted to a new treaty that forever exempted the United States from paying tribute.

1.   The word *protection* is in quotes because
     A.   piracy was called "protection" before the year 1800.
     B.   the protection of merchant ships was extremely important during the American Revolution.
     C.   England and France governed the Barbary States.
     D.   "protection" is synonymous with *pasha*.
     E.   pirates did not actually protect ships; they simply agreed to not attack them.

2.   The best substitute for the word *mutual* in line 11 is
     A.   profitable.
     B.   severe.
     C.   shared.
     D.   related.
     E.   side.

3.   United States Naval forces destroyed the *U.S.S. Philadelphia* because
     A.   they did not want the *Philadelphia* to be used as a pirate ship.
     B.   the *Philadelphia* was the most notorious ship in the pirate fleet.
     C.   they needed to prove that the United States had a sizable fleet.
     D.   the *Philadelphia* was the pasha's personal ship in the pirate fleet.
     E.   they were trying to set fire to all the pirate ships in Tripoli Harbor.

4.   As used in line 39, *terminal* most nearly means
     A.   primary.
     B.   fatal.
     C.   stopping.
     D.   worst.
     E.   strongest.

5.   The author of this passage would disagree with which of the following
      statements?
      A.   The United States Navy lacked mobility until after the War of
           1812.
      B.   In popular culture, pirates are not always associated with crime.
      C.   The Pasha of Tripoli overstepped his bounds.
      D.   Pirates looted out of necessity, not greed.
      E.   The First Barbary War failed to stop piracy.

Lesson Twenty

1. **assail** (ə sāl´) *v.* to attack physically or verbally; to assault
   While the Army *assailed* the enemy from the inland side, the Navy hit the coast.
   syn: charge   *ant: retreat; withdraw*

2. **astute** (ə stōōt´) *adj.* shrewd; keen in judgment
   The *astute* businesswoman turned failing companies into profitable organizations.
   syn: shrewd; clever   *ant: naive; ignorant*

3. **condolence** (kən dō´ləns) *n.* 1. sympathy for another's grief
                                       2. an expression of sympathy
   (1) The greeting card did not convey his *condolence* well enough.
   (2) During the funeral, friends offered *condolences* to the relatives of the deceased.
   (1) *syn: compassion; pity*   *ant: neglect; disregard*

4. **enigma** (i nig´ mə) *n.* a puzzling person or problem; a mystery
   We always regarded Greg as an *enigma*; no one ever knew his true motives.

5. **fruitless** (frōōt´ lis) *adj.* unproductive; useless
   The castaway knew that it would be *fruitless* to scream because no one could hear him.
   syn: futile; pointless   *ant: advantageous; beneficial*

6. **inexplicable** (in eks plik´ ə bəl) *adj.* impossible to explain
   Courtney could only guess as to what caused the *inexplicable* damage to her car.
   syn: baffling; mystifying   *ant: evident; obvious*

7. **malignant** (mə lig´ nənt) *adj.* 1. causing harm, suffering, or death
                                      2. evil
   (1) His *malignant* attitude disrupted the whole team.
   (2) The hero foiled the villain's *malignant* plan to take over the city.
   (1) *syn: nasty; lethal*   *ant: benign; kind*
   (2) *syn: wicked; vile*   *ant: good; kindly*

8. **monotonous** (mə not´ ə nəs) *adj.* tediously repetitious; without variety
   Treasure hunting involves many *monotonous* hours of staring at a sonar screen.
   syn: mechanical; boring   *ant: varied; exciting*

9.   **profound**   (prə found´)   *adj.*   1. emotionally or intellectually deep
                                                    2. of great intensity or reach
   (1) The author wanted his novel to have a *profound* message that
      changed the way people think about politics.
   (2) A trip to a museum can have a *profound* effect on a child.
   (1) *syn: thoughtful; weighty*   *ant: shallow; superficial*
   (2) *syn: influential; serious*   *ant: minor; insignificant*

10.   **rail**   (rāl)   *v.*   to criticize harshly
   The angry customer *railed* about the lousy service at the restaurant.
   syn: berate; rant   *ant: praise; compliment*

11.   **shun**   (shūn)   *v.*   to avoid intentionally
   Students *shunned* Brian after they learned that he was a tattle-tale.
   syn: eschew; reject   *ant: welcome; accept*

12.   **subterranean**   (sūb tə rā´ nē ən)   *adj.*   underground
   Many *subterranean* creatures, such as earthworms, have no eyes.

13.   **valor**   (val´ ər)   *n.*   bravery
   The soldier received a medal for his *valor* in combat.
   syn: courage; boldness   *ant: cowardice; fear*

14.   **variable**   (vâr´ ē ə bəl)   *adj.*   likely to change; able to be changed
                                     n.   something that is likely to change
   (adj) The fan's *variable* speed can be adjusted with the knob on the
       front.
   (n)   The many *variables* of the mission made it unsuitable for an
       inexperienced agent.
   (adj) *syn: changeable; adjustable*   *ant: constant; fixed; permanent*

15.   **virtue**   (vûr´ chōō)   *n.*   an admirable quality; moral excellence
   Each year, the town selects a person of *virtue* to be the man or woman of
   the year.
   syn: goodness; righteousness   *ant: evil; badness*

EXERCISE I – Words in Context

Using the vocabulary list for this lesson, supply the correct word to complete each sentence.

1. The chess champion tried to understand the strategy behind his opponent's _____ move.

2. The _____ accountant saved money for the company by finding various tax breaks and loopholes.

3. Friends of the deceased expressed their _____ to the surviving family members.

4. Keith took fifty pounds of loose change to the bank because he did not want the _____ job of counting it.

5. The government's secret _____ laboratory was located forty feet below the street, beneath an ordinary office building.

6. The new office chairs have _____ height settings so they can accommodate people of all sizes.

7. Ivan _____ about the company when it refused to honor the warranty on his new notebook computer.

8. His _____ efforts to find the trail simply took him farther into the jungle.

9. Patience is said to be a[n] _____, but certainly too much patience can be a fault.

10. The court declared the man innocent, but his neighbors _____ him because they no longer trusted him.

11. Losing her temper, Jenna verbally _____ the driver of the other car when he nearly caused an accident.

12. She had the _____ to confront the bully and demand that he return the child's lunch money.

13. The story is short, but it has a[n] _____ meaning.

14. The _____ growth had to be removed before it spread to other parts of the patient's body.

15. The detective struggled to solve the _____ of the missing jewelry.

EXERCISE II – Sentence Completion

Complete the sentence in a way that shows you understand the meaning of the italicized vocabulary word.

1. For *inexplicable* reasons, Ted decided to…

2. Joy's sudden change in behavior is an *enigma* because…

3. After a *fruitless* attempt to bail the water out of the boat, the captain…

4. Fishing can become *monotonous* if…

5. If you *rail* about your friend's mistake too long, your friend might…

6. In an amazing feat of *valor*, the wounded soldier…

7. The *subterranean* cavern was a good place to…

8. Some friends sent their *condolences* on sympathy cards, while others…

9. The mountain's *variable* climate made it necessary for the hikers to…

10. The knowledgeable, concerned officer had a *profound* effect on…

11. Bystanders *assailed* the mugger when…

12. Since Darren's *virtues* outnumbered his weaknesses, the boss decided to…

13. During the plague, the villagers *shunned*…

14. His love of sports became *malignant* when…

15. The *astute* collector easily determined that the antique dresser was…

EXERCISE III – Prefixes and Suffixes

Study the entries and use them to complete the questions that follow.

The suffix -*less* means "without" or "lacking"
The suffix -*ous* means "full of."
The suffix -*tic* means "pertaining to."
The suffix -*y* means "quality of" or "condition of."

Use the provided prefixes and suffixes to change each word so that it completes the sentence correctly. Then, keeping in mind that prefixes and suffixes sometimes change the part of speech, identify the part of speech of the new word by circling N for a noun, V for a verb, or ADJ for an adjective.

1. (virtue)   Not one of the _____ criminals expressed remorse for having caused the deadly accident.   N   V   ADJ

2. (enigma) Anthropologists struggled to understand the _____ disappearance of an entire ancient civilization.
   N   V   ADJ

3. (virtue) The millionaire tries to lead a[n] _____ life of kindness and charity.   N   V   ADJ

4. (monotonous) The children endured the _____ of an eight-hour drive, only to arrive at the theme park and find it closed for the day.
   N   V   ADJ

EXERCISE IV – Critical Reading

The following reading passage contains vocabulary words from this lesson. Carefully read the passage and then choose the best answers for each of the questions that follow.

1   Sometimes, it seems as though science and technology are ridding the world of its most puzzling **enigmas**, but rest assured—modern technology has yet to take us to the bottom of the Oak Island Money Pit.

2   In 1795, teenager Daniel McGinnis discovered a tree that looked as though it had been used as an anchor for a block-and-tackle, or pulley. It was a peculiar discovery because the tree stood next to a visible depression in the ground, and it was on Oak Island, one of many tiny, wooded islands in Mahone Bay, Nova Scotia. A single thought overwhelmed McGinnis: buried treasure! He quickly assembled a crew of friends and began digging. They dug to a depth of 30 feet, finding wooden platforms every 10 feet. Realizing that they would need better equipment, the team left Oak Island but agreed to return and dig further.

3   Nine years passed before the friends returned to the **inexplicable** pit. Having found someone to finance the dig, the team returned equipped as part of the Onslow Company. They descended into the hole and dug down to 90 feet, burrowing through more wooden platforms as well as layers of coconut husks, charcoal, and clay (coconuts are not native to Nova Scotia, but their fibers were common packaging material centuries ago). The team's efforts proved **fruitless** because they returned to the pit one morning to find it filled with water to the 30-foot mark, or what would be sea level. They dug another shaft parallel to the original to a depth of 110 feet. It, too, flooded, and the team surrendered; however, they claimed to have discovered a stone with strange markings at the 90-foot mark.

4   Word about Oak Island spread, and in 1849, the Truro Company re-excavated the original shaft. It flooded, so they began drilling. At 100 feet, the drill struck a wooden platform. Then it hit a layer of what appeared to be scrap metal. After passing through another three layers of wood and one of metal, the drill penetrated a 7-foot layer of clay. At one point, the drill struck what were thought to be treasure chests; links of gold allegedly were found stuck to the drill bit. In an attempt to recover the supposed chests, the Truro company dug another parallel shaft, which promptly flooded. Defeated, the team tried to determine why the pits were flooding when they made a **profound** discovery: the pit was booby-trapped. Whoever built the pit also dug a 500-foot long **subterranean** tunnel, lined with stones, that linked the pit to an artificial beach. Seawater on the beach passed through layers of grass and coconut fibers, flowed down the tunnel, and entered the pit at the 110-foot mark. This was not the work of a few

pirates quickly hiding some stolen doubloons; this was a complex project that required engineering skills, equipment, and a workforce. Someone, or some people, had built the pit for a reason. Did ancient native-Americans build it? Vikings? British Soldiers hiding riches during the American Revolution?

5   From 1861 to 1971, nine major excavations attempted to reach the unknown prize at the bottom of the pit. Successive attempts reached greater depths and found new artifacts such as work tools and a scrap of parchment, but the pit's **variable** floods and tunnel collapses bankrupted most companies before anything momentous could be found. The Money Pit was expensive in other ways, too: the pit has claimed at least six lives, leading some to believe that a **malignant** curse lingers over Oak Island.

6   During the 1971 excavation, the Triton Alliance dug to a depth of 180 feet and then dropped a television camera into a water-filled cave in the bedrock. The camera recorded what might have been man-made objects, but the shaft collapsed before divers could confirm the images. Once again, an excavation yielded no bounty but just enough evidence to inspire the next generation of treasure hunters. Two-hundred years of human advancement has failed to get us to the bottom of the Money Pit, making it one of the world's greatest mysteries.

1.   The word *inexplicable* in paragraph 3 suggests that
      A.   the Money Pit contained the answers to the curse of Oak Island.
      B.   no one knew why the pit became flooded with water.
      C.   Daniel McGinnis needed to solve the mystery of the Money Pit.
      D.   the origins of the pit were not yet known to anyone.
      E.   discovering the pit was an unforgettable experience.

2.   According to paragraph 4, the Money Pit was probably not built by pirates because
      A.   Daniel McGinnis constructed the Money Pit with his friends.
      B.   pirates had neither the resources nor the reasons to undertake such a task.
      C.   only the British army possessed the required engineering skills.
      D.   the Money Pit predates the pirates by nearly two centuries.
      E.   pirates seldom visited the North American coast.

3.   The best substitute for the word *variable* in paragraph 5 would be
      A.   unpredictable.
      B.   inflexible.
      C.   unwavering.
      D.   discouraging.
      E.   indirect.

4. Which of the following was *not* reported to have been found in the Money Pit?
    A. charcoal
    B. parchment
    C. doubloons
    D. coconut fibers
    E. scrap metal

5. Which choice does not describe one of the themes of the passage?
    A. the human obsession with treasure
    B. overconfidence in technology
    C. the human attraction to the unknown
    D. the allegiance of friendship
    E. superstition based in reality

Lesson Twenty-One

1. **aspire** (ə spīr´) *v.* to desire strongly; to seek something great
    The teacher told the students to *aspire* to their greatest dreams, no matter how distant they seemed to be.
    syn: pursue; strive   *ant: reject; dismiss*

2. **composure** (kəm pō´ zhər) *n.* calmness of mind, especially while under stress
    In a fire, keep your *composure* and do not panic.
    syn: serenity; tranquility; cool   *ant: panic; agitation*

3. **deploy** (di ploi´) *v.* to distribute strategically and put into action
    The Army *deployed* troops to protect the truck convoy.
    syn: position; marshal   *ant: recall; withdraw*

4. **exonerate** (ig zon´ ə rāt) *v.* to clear of blame
    DNA evidence *exonerated* the suspect in the murder case.
    syn: absolve; acquit   *ant: incriminate; charge*

5. **exploit** (ek´ sploit [n.] orek sploit´ [v.]) *n.* an adventure; an achievement
    v. to use to one's advantage
    (n) The treasure hunter published a book that detailed his many *exploits*.
    (v) The agency *exploited* her mathematical talents to decipher the enemy's secret code.

6. **flamboyant** (flam boi´ ənt) *adj.* decorated to excess; ornate
    All the guests stared in amazement at the host's *flamboyant* suit; it was red, shiny silk, and covered with rhinestones and decorative embroidery.
    syn: flashy; garish   *ant: plain; simple*

7. **fret** (fret´) *v.* to worry
    Cara's parents constantly *fretted* about their daughter while she was at summer camp.
    syn: anguish; fuss   *ant: relax*

8. **hostile** (hos´ təl) *adj.* 1. showing ill will; unfriendly
    2. unfavorable to life or well-being
    (1) The explorers hoped to avoid any confrontations with *hostile* natives.
    (2) Many of the colonists did not survive the *hostile* winter.
    syn: antagonistic; adverse   *ant: pleasant; welcoming*

9. **lackluster** (lak´ lus tər) *adj.* lacking brilliance or vitality
The actor's *lackluster* performance disappointed the audience.
syn: dull; bland   *ant: radiant; dazzling*

10. **maternal** (mə tûr´ nəl) *adj.* 1. motherly
2. related or inherited through one's mother
(1) Her *maternal* instinct caused her to check on the sleeping children.
(2) Everyone thought that Joe shared his hair color with his *maternal* grandfather.

11. **morose** (mə rōs´) *adj.* sad; gloomy
Annette was *morose* for days after her dog died.
syn: depressed; sullen   *ant: cheerful; merry*

12. **procrastinate** (prō kras´tə nāt) *v.* to delay needlessly
Irene had a month to write the essay, but she *procrastinated* until the night before it was due.
syn: postpone; put off   *ant: hasten; rush*

13. **replenish** (ri plen´ ish) *v.* to make full or complete again
The waiter *replenished* the empty salt and pepper shakers on the tables.
syn: refill; reload   *ant: exhaust; deplete*

14. **saga** (sä´ gə) *n.* a narrative tale
There is a three-part *saga* on television about the experiences of a famous explorer.
syn: chronicle; epic

15. **static** (sta´ tik) *adj.* motionless; inactive; fixed
The terrible event did not seem to affect Ben's *static* personality.
syn: unchanging; stationary   *ant: changing; unstable;*
                                                dynamic

EXERCISE I – Words in Context

Using the vocabulary list for this lesson, supply the correct word to complete each sentence.

1. The news media are sometimes said to _____ tragedies to get good ratings.

2. The _____ crowd threw food at the comedian when it heard his controversial routine.

3. The _____ movie depressed us more than it entertained us.

4. Astronauts must be able to maintain their _____ during the most extreme situations.

5. "Don't _____ about the little things; everything will be fine," said Grandpa.

6. The old dog exhibited _____ instincts and cared for the abandoned puppies as though they were her own.

7. Uncle Bob's _____ about the worst day of his life was interesting the first time, but not the second or third.

8. Since you _____, you will have to work all night to finish the job by tomorrow.

9. The _____ actress wore thousand-dollar shoes to the grocery store.

10. He _____ to become a rock star despite his obvious lack of talent.

11. An array of huge, _____ cables supports the massive weight of the highway bridge across the canyon.

12. Please _____ the paper towels if you use the last one.

13. The creative editor transforms _____ manuscripts into exciting, bestselling novels.

14. The governor _____ National Guard troops to the city to suppress the riot.

15. Once the real thief was caught, the court _____ the man originally jailed for the crime.

EXERCISE II – Sentence Completion

Complete the sentence in a way that shows you understand the meaning of the italicized vocabulary word.

1. During the first part of the *saga*, the main character...

2. No matter how much she studies, Gayle always *frets* about...

3. The park service installed a *static* cable along the steep trail to help...

4. The city *deployed* dozens of workers to pick up trash after...

5. The owners of the mansion *exploited* its historic significance by...

6. To improve the looks of her *lackluster* apartment, Donna...

7. Her *flamboyant* clothes made her stand out in the crowd because...

8. When she saw the child's *morose* expression, the woman asked...

9. Ben usually *procrastinates*, so he probably will not even begin the project until...

10. Her father's side of the family is easygoing, but her *maternal* relatives are...

11. It is difficult to keep your *composure* when...

12. If no one *replenishes* the campfire with firewood, we might...

13. If you suddenly find yourself in a *hostile* situation, you should...

14. She tried to *exonerate* herself by finding...

15. She *aspired* to become...

EXERCISE III – Prefixes and Suffixes

Study the entries and use them to complete the questions that follow.

The prefix *dis-* means "not" or "apart."
The prefix *re-* means "back" or "again."
The suffix *-ation* means "act of" or "result of."
The suffix *-ful* means "full of" or "having."

Use the provided prefixes and suffixes to change each word so that it completes the sentence correctly. Then, keeping in mind that prefixes and suffixes sometimes change the part of speech, identify the part of speech of the new word by circling N for a noun, V for a verb, or ADJ for an adjective.

1. (aspire) Her greatest _____ in life is to become a famous scientist.

    N   V   ADJ

2. (composure) He spoke well during the interview, but his shaking hands revealed his _____.   N   V   ADJ

3. (fret) The _____ actress was so nervous that she could barely speak.

    N   V   ADJ

4. (deploy) If the enemy attacks the weaker part of the front line, the general will _____ the troops to that area.

    N   V   ADJ

EXERCISE IV – Improving Paragraphs

Read the following passage and then answer the multiple-choice questions that follow. The questions will require you to make decisions regarding the revision of the reading selection.

1   Do not **fret** if you cannot tell Bach from Beethoven. After this short lesson in Western classical music history, you will be able to keep your **composure** and perhaps even answer correctly if someone asks whether the music playing on the elevator intercom is Baroque or Classical.

2   The birth of modern music occurred during the Middle Ages (450–1450) as *monophonic* music gradually evolved into *polyphonic* music. Monophonic music, such as Gregorian chant, had a single, unaccompanied melody and a delicate rhythm, if any at all. Musicians experimented with mixed voices, both human and instrumental, and new instruments such as the lute, the shawm (an early oboe), and the trombone. Secular, or non-religious, music grew in popularity, and throughout the Renaissance (1450–1600), small groups of musicians performed, often as quartets of like-sounding instruments.

3   During the Baroque musical era (1600–1750), science and exploration became powerful influences, and musicians refined music to the limits of established boundaries. Continuous bass accompaniment became a musical standard, and complex, repeating, polyphonic melodies made Renaissance music seem **lackluster** by comparison. The inventions of the harpsichord and clavichord enabled virtuosos such as J. S. Bach to demonstrate extremely complex yet supremely ordered music. Basically a harp laid flat and played using a pianolike keyboard that plucks the strings, the harpsichord contributed a distinct twanging sound to Baroque music, and music written for churches often switched to the organ instead of the harpsichord. To identify Baroque music, listen for a harpsichord, a **static** tempo, and complex, interwoven melodies.

4   From 1825 to 1900, science, nature, and the supernatural combined to create **flamboyant** musical extremes. Composers **aspired** to write emotional music; tempos accelerated and music rang with bold, nationalistic themes that celebrated the spirit of revolution. Operas, such as those by Richard Wagner, echoed timeless **sagas** through powerful brass instruments across wide musical ranges. Other music featured exotic, new instruments such as the tuba and the saxophone. The modern symphony orchestra was established, and compositions often featured master pianists or other instrumentalists exhibiting their skills. Listen for modern instruments and emotional, musical extremes as indicators of Romantic music.

5   Machines and factories held the world's attention during the eighteenth century, and Classical composers (1750–1825) wrestled with the

fascination by creating music with themes of art and nature; however, music did not escape the Industrial Revolution. Symphonies—long, multiple-part compositions made famous by Joseph Hayden, Wolfgang Mozart, and later Ludwig van Beethoven—had the structure, control, and balance of an efficient factory. Classical music emphasized control over emotional extremes, and it was largely *homophonic*, or of a single, accompanied melody. Orchestras grew to accommodate composers' musical **exploits**. The piano also emerged, just in time to become a perfect outlet for talent during the upcoming "Age of the Virtuoso," or Romantic era.

6   As the Romantic age gave way to the contemporary era, traditional rules of composition went out the window. No single musical style dominates modern music, and there is widespread debate over whether certain compositions are even music at all. Some contemporary composers, such as Igor Stravinsky, Richard Strauss, and Aaron Copland, created popular masterworks by combining Romantic trends with modern techniques. Other composers, however, sought completely new musical forms through random rhythms, clashing sounds, and unpredictable melodies, all of which consequently make later contemporary classical music easy to identify.

1.   Which sentence should be added after the following first two sentences of paragraph 2?

> The birth of modern music occurred during the Middle Ages (450–1450) as *monophonic* music gradually evolved into *polyphonic* music. Monophonic music, such as Gregorian chant, had a single, unaccompanied melody and a delicate rhythm, if any at all.

     A.   Gregorian chant would be an example of monophonic music.
     B.   Polyphonic music featured multiple melodies playing simultaneously.
     C.   Monophonic music replaced polyphonic music altogether.
     D.   Polyphonic music is more complex.
     E.   But monophonic music would soon lay the foundation for the Baroque era.

2. Which choice best revises the underlined portion of the following sentence from paragraph 3?

> Basically a harp laid flat and played using a pianolike keyboard that plucks the strings, the harpsichord contributed a distinct twanging sound to Baroque <u>music, and music written for churches often switched to the organ instead of the harpsichord.</u>

A. music. Because of this, music written for churches substituted an organ for the harpsichord.
B. music—music written for churches substituted an organ for the harpsichord.
C. music; however, music written for churches substituted a harpsichord for the organ.
D. music. And music written for churches switched to the organ instead of the harpsichord.
E. music, though church music often substituted an organ for the harpsichord.

3. Which choice would best improve the organization of the whole passage?
A. Delete paragraphs 1 and 6.
B. Exchange paragraphs 4 and 5.
C. Include more references to famous composers.
D. Move paragraph 2 to follow paragraph 6.
E. Explain the dual use of the word *classical* throughout the passage.

4. Adding which information would improve the essay without distracting from the main idea?
A. the effects of music therapy on stress levels
B. the lives of famous medieval musicians
C. key characteristics that identify music from the Classical period
D. how modern rock and jazz compare to classical music
E. the evolution of music from the Stone Age to the Renaissance

Review

Lessons 19 – 21

EXERCISE I – Inferences

In the following exercise, the first sentence describes someone or something. Infer information from the first sentence, and then choose the word from the Word Bank that best completes the second sentence.

Word Bank

hostile	variable	lackluster	indifferent
profound	lucid	mutual	fruitless

1. Joy likes camping, but Zach would rather stay in a hotel.
   From this sentence, we can infer that Joy and Zach do not have a(n)_____ fondness for camping.

2. The popular book led many people to change their lifestyles or question their whole existence.
   From this sentence, we can infer that the book has a[n] _____ effect on some people.

3. The crowd booed and hissed and yelled threats at the comedian when she told a particularly offensive joke.
   From this sentence, we can infer that the crowd became _____.

4. Norman knew little about style or trends; he simply wore whichever clothes were not in the dirty laundry pile.
   From this sentence, we can infer that Norman is _____ about fashion.

5. By turning the knob, a listener can adjust the volume on the stereo.
   From this sentence, we can infer that the volume of the stereo is _____.

EXERCISE II – Related Words

Some of the vocabulary words from lessons 19–21 have related meanings. Complete the following sentences by choosing the word that best completes the specified relationship. Some word pairs will be antonyms, some will be synonyms, and some will be words often used in the same context.

1. *Replenish* is closest in meaning to
    A. retort.
    B. rail.
    C. fret.
    D. deploy.
    E. bolster.

2. If parts of a message are not *lucid*, then the reason for the message might be
    A. flamboyant.
    B. inexplicable.
    C. adverse.
    D. subterranean.
    E. maternal.

3. If something is *adverse* to the forces of good, then it is
    A. fruitless.
    B. morose.
    C. malignant.
    D. mutual.
    E. indifferent.

4. If an intentional statement has a *profound* effect on someone, then the speaker's effort was not
    A. fruitless.
    B. lucid.
    C. astute.
    D. terminal.
    E. morose.

5. Listening to a *lackluster* speech can quickly become
    A. quaint.
    B. hostile.
    C. static.
    D. terminal.
    E. monotonous.

6. *Static* has the opposite meaning of
   A. blunder.
   B. aspire.
   C. variable.
   D. exploit.
   E. inexplicable.

7. *Rail* has roughly the same meaning as
   A. fret.
   B. assail.
   C. procrastinate.
   D. bolster.
   E. shun.

8. A person living a *flamboyant* lifestyle would not want to live in a[n]
   _____ house.
   A. subterranean
   B. profound
   C. brazen
   D. quaint
   E. astute

9. *Valor* is normally regarded as a kind of
   A. enigma.
   B. condolence.
   C. saga.
   D. virtue.
   E. blunder.

10. In an *alliance*, both of the sides have at least some _____ interests.
    A. mutual
    B. maternal
    C. brazen
    D. hostile
    E. terminal

EXERCISE III – Crossword Puzzle

Use the clues to complete the crossword puzzle. The answers consist of vocabulary words from lessons 19 through 21.

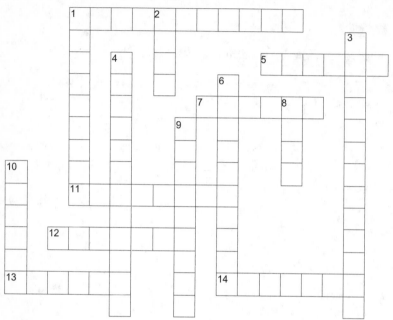

Across

1. The noise from the construction site bothers some people, but Steve is _____ to it.
5. When Jill pointed out an obvious flaw, Susan's _____ was a sarcastic "Thanks a lot."
7. Elizabeth becomes _____ whenever she reads about the misfortunes of others.
11. On its _____ voyage, the Titanic struck an iceberg and sank.
12. Kate failed the audition when she _____ [ed] while reading her lines.
13. The museum's surveillance camera recorded nothing unusual, so the disappearance of the mummy was a[n] _____.
14. The settlers decided to _____ the river by using it to transport lumber and coal to the city.

Down

1. The new government battled _____ forces trying to restore their former general to power.
2. Lee _____[s] about being attacked by wild animals every time she goes camping.
3. The longer you _____ in seeing a doctor, the harder it will be to fix what is wrong.
4. The bank's _____ vault sits fifty feet below the basement parking garage.
6. Friends offered _____[s] to Mike when they learned about his recent loss.
8. When someone commits a crime in the small village, the inhabitants _____ the offender for one year.
9. The new evidence will _____ the wrongfully accused woman.
10. The _____ tourist quickly realized that she was about to become the next victim of a scam.